S0-BZT-234

hawkeye

VOLUME 2

MATT FRACTION
WRITER

HAWKEYE #13, #15, #19 & #21-22

DAVID AJA
ARTIST/COVERS

MATT HOLLINGSWORTH
COLOR ARTIST

HAWKEYE #12

FRANCESCO FRANCAVILLA
ARTIST/COLORS/COVER

HAWKEYE #17

CHRIS ELIOPOULOS
WITH DAVID AJA (PP. 1 & 20)
ARTISTS

JORDIE BELLAIRE
COLOR ARTIST

DAVID AJA
COVER ART

HAWKEYE ANNUAL #1

JAVIER PULIDO
ARTIST/COVER

MATT HOLLINGSWORTH
COLOR ARTIST

HAWKEYE #14, #16, #18 & #20

ANNIE WU
ARTIST

MATT HOLLINGSWORTH
COLOR ARTIST

DAVID AJA
COVER ART

CHRIS ELIOPOULOS (#1-22) WITH DAVID AJA (#19) & CLAYTON COWLES (ANNUAL #1)
LETTERERS

DEVIN LEWIS
ASSISTANT EDITOR

TOM BRENNAN
ASSOCIATE EDITOR

STEPHEN WACKER & SANA AMANAT
EDITORS

17

clint barton, a.k.a.

hawkeye

'twas in hawkeye #6, on the last page of the book,
clint watched christmas cartoons--no really, go look.
now it's your turn to see hawkguy's new winter friends,
and how they react when evil descends!
why are you still reading this improvised rhyme?
this is the greatest comic ever--stop wasting time!

clint barton
(hawkeye)
avenger

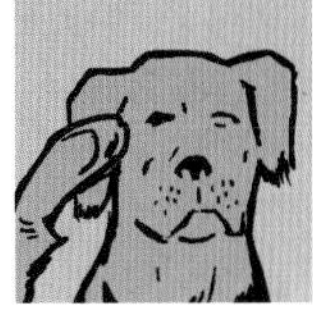

lucky
(pizza dog)

CLINT...?

SORRY. JUST--

YEAH. OKAY. WHAT ARE WE DOING?
WATCHING "WINTER FRIENDS."

WHAT ONE IS THAT, AGAIN?
"WINTER FRIENDS."

WHAT?

"WINTER FRIENDS."

IS THAT THE ONE WITH SANTA?
NOPE.

THEN WHO?

"WINTER FRIENDS."

SIMONE, IS THE-- AHH.

ZRK
FFRF

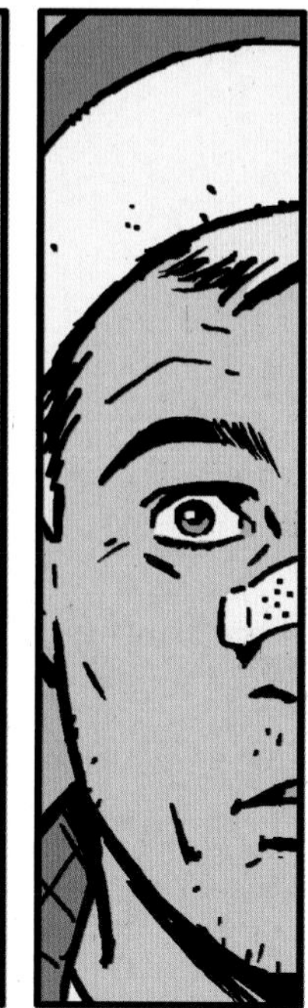

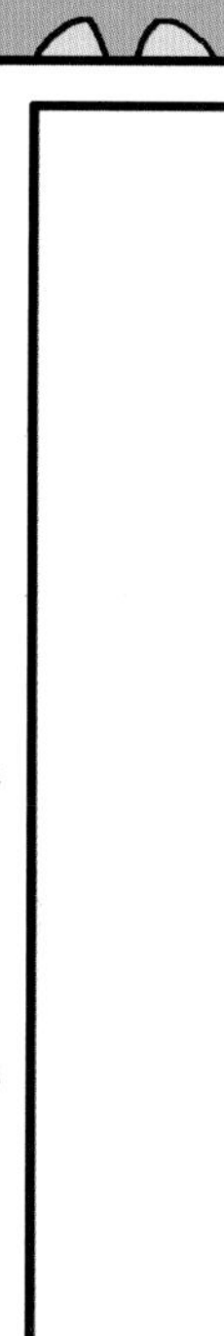

THE mbc WINTERTIME WINTER FRIENDS WINTER FUN SPECIAL
WINTERTIME'S THE BEST
BETTER THAN THE REST
SNOWBALL FIGHTS
SHINING LIGHTS
AND MULTIDENOMENATIONAL
PANTHEISTIC ALL-INCLUSIVE
SEASONAL FESTS
GETTIN' PURDY HOT OUT HERE, FELLERS...
ACK, SNOWY'S RIGHT.
I COULD USE A COLD DRINK...
HERRRPPPLLGG MMEHHHH
OOPH!
IT'S HOT LIKE SUMMER!
OH NO-- SNOWY!
GLLRG
MY NIGHTMARES ARE TURNING REAL!!
HE'S DYING!
GLACK
THIS LOOKS LIKE A JOB FOR THE...
WINTER FRIENDS!

IF IT'S COLD OUTSIDE AND TROUBLE'S ON THE RISE, CHILDREN OF EVERY SHAPE AND SIZE AROUND THE WORLD CAN ALWAYS RELY ON THEIR ONE AND ONLY--
YALDOG!
PROUD POOCH OF POWER REPRESENTING THE PERSIAN HOLIDAY YALDA!
RAMA-IN-PAJAMAS!
THIS HINDU DEITY IS DOWN WITH DIWALI! AND IS ALSO A LLAMA!
SANTALOPE!
HO HO HO BOY, MAKE WAY FOR THIS YULETIDE TITAN!
SAMANTHA HAIN, THE PAGAN PRINCESS!
JUST LIKE THE SCARY GIRL ALWAYS "READING" "ALONE" IN THE "LIBARRY!"
KWANZAAGATOR!
CHAMPION CHOMPER OF ALL THE FRUITS OF THE HARVEST!
MENORABLE!
NINE LIVES! NINE CANDLES! L'CHAIM!
WINTER FRIENDS!

YALDOG, WHY IS IT SO HOT?
I DON'T KNOW, SANTALOPE! WHY DO I FEEL SO WEAK?
DON'T YOU SEE, FELLOW WINTER FRIENDS?
WITHOUT THE COLD NO ONE NEEDS OUR HOLIDAY REMINDERS OF SURVIVAL AND KINSHIP AND WARMTH!
WE'RE POWERLESS!
ONLY A MONSTER LIKE THAT COULD HAVE TURNED WINTER INTO SUMMERLIKE THIS!!
HEY, GUYS. HOWAREYA?
A NAP PROBABLY SOUNDS REAL GOOD RIGHT ABOUT NOW, HUH?
NOOOOOO!
HE'S... RIGHT...
OH...NO...
THIS MEANS OUR...ONLY HOPE IS...

"...STEVE, THE DOG WITH NO POWERS THAT WE LET HANG OUT WITH US ALL FOR SOME REASON."
WF
!
WHO SAID MY NAME?
SOMEONE SOMEWHERE SAID MY NAME?
WHO SAID "STEVE"?!
COSTUMES
IF SOMEBODY SAID MY NAME IT COULD MEAN THE WINTER FRIENDS ARE IN TROUBLE!
I BETTERRF...
FFFWIPP INTFFO
MY FFFUPERHERO COFFTUME--
KNOCK KNOCK

OH BOY
OH BOY
OH BOY
OH BOY
OH BOY IT'S--
WF
WF
HEY! HI! STEVE! IT'S ME!
AWW, LIL...
HEY, STEVE, DID YOU HEAR SOMEONE SAY YOUR NAME? I HEARD SOMEONE SAY YOUR NAME AND I THOUGHT
"WELL IF I JUST HEARD SOMEONE SAY STEVE'S NAME I BET STEVE HEARD SOMEONE SAY HIS NAME AND THAT COULD MEAN ADVENTURE--"
UGH.
CHOMP
AAOWHATWAS THAT FOR?
EEEFFF, LIL, YERR FFUCH A SPAFFFZZZZH
OH BOY OH BOY COSTUME TIME! TIME FOR STEVE AND LIL TO SUIT UP AND--
I CAN DO IT ALL BY MYSELF!
YIPE!

HEY, BRUDDER!
I JUST HEARD SOMEBODY SAY "STEVE"!
AW, BRUDDER--
SLURRP
--WHO'S MY BRUDDER--
SLURRP
--WHAT A GOOD BRUDDER YOU ARE BRUDDER--
HI, HERMAN.
ARE WE GONNA GO HAVE AN ADVENTURE NOW?
I LOVE ADVENTURE! WE'RE ADVENTURE BRUDDERS!
YIP YAP YAP YAP YIP YIP
BRUDDDDDERRRR!
GGRRRRRR
BRUDDER BRUDDER BRUDDER BRUDDER
STEVE STEVE STEVE STEVE STEVE STEVE
I CAN DO IT ALL BY MYSELF!

AD-VEN-TURE,
AD-VEN-TURE!
AD-VEN-TURE,
AD-VEN-TURE!
AD-VEN-TURE,
AD-VEN-TURING
WITH STEVE!
GRRRR...
HEY, BOSSMAN, CHEER UP! WE'RE ON AN ADVENTURE, WHAT BAD COULD POSSIBLY HAP--?
BONK
UH-OH...
HEY, DOG...
UGH, I HATE THESE GUYS...
YOU DOGS IN WRONG PART OF WOODS, DOG.
YEAH, DOG.
DOG.

DINGOES GET THOSE DOGS, DOGS!
DOG THOSE DOGS ARE DEAD, DOGS!
WAIT, WHAT?
GRRR
WHY I OUGHTA--
SNIP
DANG IT, DINGOES!
CHOMP!
DOG!

THUD!
TAKE THAT, DOG.
NOT EVEN REAL WINTER FRIEND, DOG. YOU GOT NO WINTER CELEBRATION POWERS, DOG.
DOG, YOU JUST DOG, DOG.
YIP!
YIP!
YIP!
YIP!
YIP!
DOG!
DOG!
DOG!
DOG!
HEY! DINGO!
DON'T YOU DARE SHE'S JUST A--
THIS LOOKS REALLY BAD, YOU GUYS...!
HA! YOU DOGS SO DUMB DOGS! YOU GOT NO POWERS, DOG! YOU GOT NO FRIENDS--
ZATZ!

BACK OFF, YA BUNCHA DUMB DINGOES!
UNLESS YOU WANT ANOTHER TASTE OF DOG JUSTICE.
OR GET AGAIN MORE OF THE ZOTZER... IS FINE FOR ME EITHER WAY.
NEED A HAND, HERMAN?
DOG!
YOU SAID IT, BIRDIE...
AND YOU, DINGO, TASTE BITE OF SPOOKY.
AAOOW DOG, WHAT WE EVER DO TO YOU DOGS, DOG?
HEY! HEY! HEY! HEY! HEY!
LEAVE MY FRIEND...DOG... ALONE!
LADY, DANG IT...
I CAN DO IT ALL BY MYSELF!

TO HECK WITH THIS, DOG.
OWW, DOG.
DOG, THOSE DOGS ARE CRAZY DOGS, DOG.
NOW WHAT WAS ALL THIS NONSENSE ABOUT YOU BEING ABLE TO HANDLE THIS ADVENTURE BY YOURSELF, STEVE?
I CAN...
NO.
...DO IT ALL...
NO.
BY MYSELF?
NO YOU CAN NOT.
HEY, GUYS, AM I CRAZY OR IS IT GETTING CRAZY HOT OUT HERE?
I THOUGHT IT WAS OUR COSTUMES AND ALL THE FIGHTING BUT LILLY'S RIGHT, LADIES.
SO I BET I REALLY DID HEAR SOMEONE CALL MY NAME. I BET IT WAS THE WINTER FRIENDS--
--AND I BET THEY'RE REALLY IN TROUBLE!
YOU ALL STAY HERE AND BE HOT--
EXCUSE ME?
I'M GOING TO THE PALACE OF THE SUN TO RESCUE THE WINTER FRIENDS...
...ALL BY MYSELF!

HEFF
HEFF
PANT!
PANT!
OW OW WARM PAWS WARM--
YIIIIIIIIKES!!
ALL RIGHT, PALACE OF THE SUN...
TIME FOR YOU TO COOL IT.
HA HA! GREAT ONE, STEVE.
THANKS, STEVE.

IT'S SUMMER! AND I'M SO HAPPY! IT'S TOO WARM FOR SNOWBALL FIGHTS AND PLOWS!
BECAUSE IT'S SUMMER! SO WARM AND SUNNY! THE WINTER FRIENDS CAN'T SAVE THE SOLSTICE NOW!
YES IT'S SUMMER! AND I'M A GENIUS! IT'S SUMMER TIME THAT ALL THE SCHOOL KIDS LOVE!
SO LET'S HAVE SOLSTICE! IN THE SUNSHINE! AND THROW AWAY OUR COATS AND BOOTS AND GLOVES!
SUMMER RULES! WINTER DROO--
PIFF!

HEY, MISTER SUN--
THE JERK STORE FAXED--
--AND THEY DON'T LIKE YOU AT ALL!
WHAT? THAT DOESN'T EVEN MAKE--
--OOPH!
HI-YAH!
UH, STEVE?
THAT GUY IS, LIKE, THE ICON OF SUMMERTIME ITSELF AND YOU'RE JUST STANDING ON HIS CHEST BARKING AT HIM...
YOU'RE KIND OF OUT OF YOUR LEAGUE, BUDDY...
I MEAN WE LOVE YA AND ALL, BUT...
BARK!
BARK!
BARK!
GRRRRR...
BAD DOG.
BAD!
DOG!
YOU'RE NOT EVEN A REAL WINTER FRIEND....!

HA HA! HOT DOG!
GET IT?
FASH!
"STEVE THE DOG"? MORE LIKE STEVE THE--
ZAPF!
'FRAIDY CAT!
I MEAN, SERIOUSLY, WHO ARE YOU, EVEN?
ZRAK!
I'M THE DOG THAT KNOWS YOU DON'T JUST GET TO DO WHATEVER JUST BECAUSE YOU WANT!
YIPE!
SHOOM!
I'M THE DOG THAT SAYS NO TO JERKS LIKE YOU FOR EVERYBODY ELSE TOO AFRAID TO SAY IT!
AND I'LL NEVER STOP BARKING JUST BECAUSE YOU FORGOT THE WAY THE WORLD SHOULD WORK!
ZAPP!
I DON'T CARE IF I'M NOT A WINTER FRIEND. I'M NOT GONNA LEAVE ANYBODY ALONE AGAINST A BIG BULLY JERK LIKE YOU!
FZARK!

!
AND NEITHER WILL WE.
JERK!
FOOLS!
I ALREADY BEAT THE WINTER FRIENDS ONCE! WHAT MAKES YOU THINK I CAN'T BEAT THE WINTER FRIENDS AND A BUNCH OF DUMB DOGS IN COSTUMES?!
NOBODY'S CELEBRATING ANY OF YOUR PRECIOUS WINTER CELEBRATIONS RIGHT NOW.
SO WHAT CAN YOU POSSIBLY DO NOW, IN MY OWN PALACE, THAT THEY COULDN'T DO?
THE REASON ANY OF US HAVE POWER IS BECAUSE SO MANY PEOPLE COME TOGETHER IN THE FACE OF DARKNESS.
PEOPLE FROM ALL OVER REACH OUT TO ONE ANOTHER AND HOLD ON AGAINST THE LONG DARK COLD TOGETHER.
SO WE'RE GOING TO DO WHAT WE ALWAYS DO.
WE'RE GONNA COME TOGETHER AND ASK FOR A LITTLE BACKUP...

HELLO, CHILDREN--

--DID SOMEONE CALL MY NAME?

MOTHER WINTER...!

NO MA'AM, NO, NOPE, NOBODY CALLED YOU HERE, NOBODY AT ALL I SWEAR--

PLEASE DON'T FREEZE ME!

WELL NOW. ARE YOU STEVE?

YES, UH.

YES, MA'AM.

GOOD DOG.

OH! HEY, STEVE!
AREN'T YOU GONNA JOIN US AT OUR FESTIVAL TO CELEBRATE ALL MULTIDENOMENATIONAL PANTHEISTIC ALL-INCLUSIVE SEASONAL FESTIVALS...?
UH, YEAH. THAT'S ME.
PARTYING DOWN.
YEAH, YOU'RE A REAL PARTY ANIMAL THERE, GUY...
YOU PARTY DOWN FOR ME, LILLY, OKAY?
I COULDN'T HAVE DONE IT WITHOUT YOU.
IF ANYBODY HAD GOTTEN HURT, I'D NEVER FORGIVE MYSELF.
THANK YOU.
AWW, WE MAKE A GREAT TEAM!
LILLY-AND-STEVE!
STEVE AND LIL.
LILLY-AND-STEVE!

S'OVER, MOMMA.
YYYAAAAWWN.
DID EVERYONE THANK CLIN--

AWW, LOOK AT THAT.

JOYOUS KWANZAA, CLINT BARTON.
THANK YOU FOR TAKING CARE OF US.

CLICK

MMMFRMM...

12

barney barton, the brother of hawkeye

traded on his brother's name once upon a time.

long story short, he was a fake avenger and it worked out about as well as you'd think.

he's been a carnie, a crook, an f.b.i. agent, a victim and a villain.

when clint last saw him, he'd donated bone marrow to save his brother's eyesight.

also clint might have stolen a whole lot of money from him.

clint barton
(hawkeye)

barney barton
(trick shot)

HEY, GUESS WHAT?
CHICKENBUTT.
A LITTLE WHILE. I DUNNO. YOU SPARE THE PRICE OF A CUPPA COFFEE FOR A FELLOW AMERICAN DOWN ON HIS LUCK OR WHAT?
3
5
NAH, I DON'T WANT NONE'A THAT BUSINESS. HOW 'BOUT TOMORROW, NINE?
CLICK
9
#
OKAY.

BZZZZ
BARTO

BZZZ

BZZZ

AHH, CLINT.

BZZZ

BZZZ
BZZZ

MORNIN'.

MORNIN'.

SPARE CHANGE?

WORTH A SHOT.

BRO.

BRO, SERIOUSLY.

SERIOUSLY, BRO. HE COME TO *OUR* VAN, BRO?

HEY THERE, GUYS, AHH...

SPARE CHANGE?

BRO. **SERIOUSLY,** BRO.

CHANGE? BRO, I GIVE YOU WHOLE DOLLAR, BRO...

...IF YOU LET ME PUNCH IN *FACE.*

FIVE DOLLARS.

C'MON, BUTTERCUP, TAKE YOUR SHOT.

FUUFFH. OKAY.
FIVE DOLLARS.

HEY--

ROWF
ROWF

ROWF
ROWF
ARROW?!

...RIP-OFF.

SEVENTEEN, EIGHTEEN...

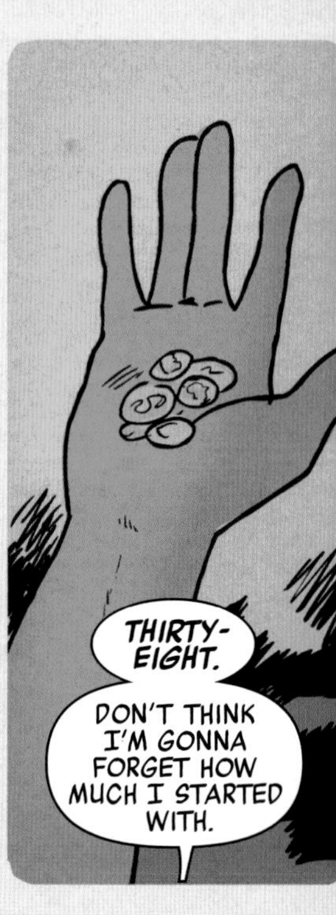
THIRTY-EIGHT.
DON'T THINK I'M GONNA FORGET HOW MUCH I STARTED WITH.

NO, CLINT--
CLINT--

DON'T TAKE THE DIMES. IT'S EASIER BUT THEY'RE TOO SMALL.

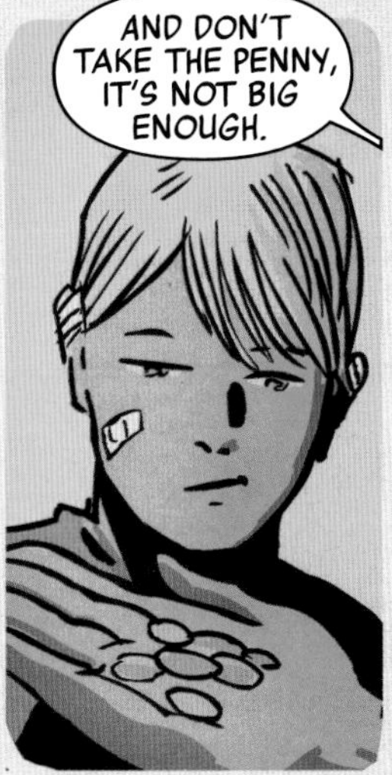
AND DON'T TAKE THE PENNY, IT'S NOT BIG ENOUGH.

YOU NEED A NICKEL.
IN GOD WE TRUST
LIBERTY
1942

IT'S NOT ENOUGH TO JUST SNAP IT, YOU GOTTA--

SNAP!

CRASH!!

ARMS AND WRIST, OKAY? YOU GOTTA SNAP AND THROW ALL AT ONCE.

SNAP!

DING

HEY, AT LEAST YOU **HIT IT,** YOU JUST GOTTA GET **STRONGER** NOW, S'ALL.

BOYYYYYS!!!

GET IN THE DAMN HOUSE **NOW!**

"THE IDENTIFIED PATIENT."
FFHH.

I GOTTA PAY SOME CEDAR FALLS CANDY-ASS THREE HUNDRED DOLLARS TO SAY YOU'RE "THE IDENTIFIED PATIENT," HRRR.

I OUGHTA TAKE THAT THREE HUNNERT OUT OF YOUR ASS, BOY.

CLINT...

YOU DUMBASS.

--IT'S OKAY, IT'S OKAY, IT'S JUST ME...

OLD MAN'S PASSED OUT. HERE.
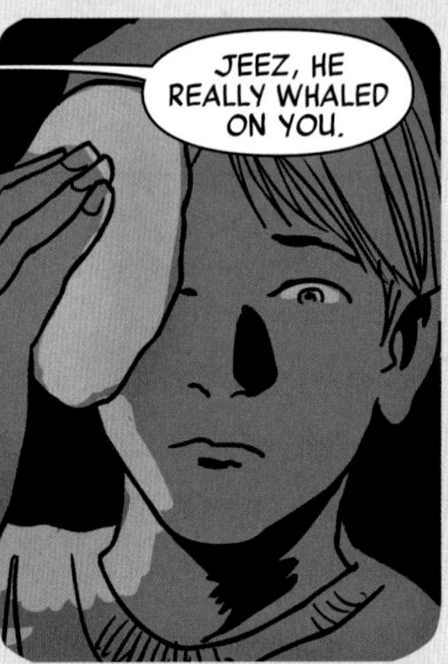
JEEZ, HE REALLY WHALED ON YOU.

IT'S NOT THAT YOU AIN'T BRAVE, BUT YOU'RE JUST TOO LITTLE.
YOU NEED TO GET STRONG BEFORE YOU DO CRAZY STUFF LIKE THAT.

HERE.

PUNCH ME.

IT'S OKAY.
I CAN TAKE IT.

YYEEOOOW!!

IT'S OKAY.
I'M OKAY.

SEE? GREAT AIM.
GOT ME RIGHT IN THE NOSE.

'KAY, GET UP.

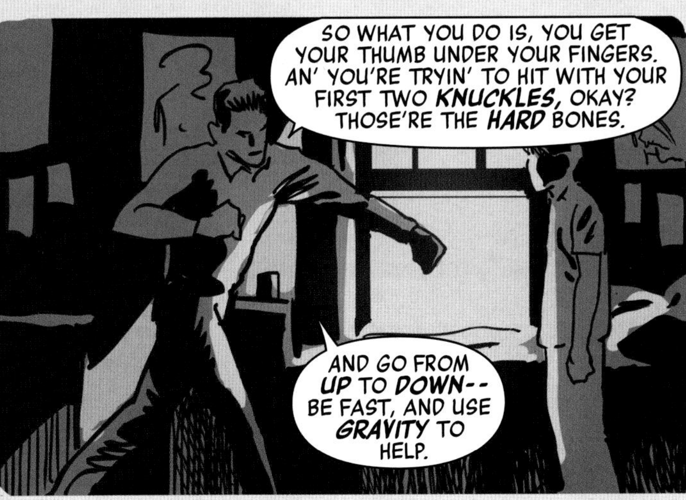
SO WHAT YOU DO IS, YOU GET YOUR THUMB UNDER YOUR FINGERS. AN' YOU'RE TRYIN' TO HIT WITH YOUR FIRST TWO KNUCKLES, OKAY? THOSE'RE THE HARD BONES.
AND GO FROM UP TO DOWN-- BE FAST, AND USE GRAVITY TO HELP.

PUT YOUR WHOLE BODY BEHIND IT. USE YOUR LEGS. AND LAUNCH AT ME.

WELL?
C'MON.

GUUURKKK

GUH.
GUH.
GUESS WHAT?

CHICKENBUTT.
AGAIN.

BRO.
TWO MINUTES, BRO.

AND YOU GET THIS.

TWO MINUTES.
AN' HELP ME UP.

AHAHA

HA HA

HAHAHA

HEY!

YOUR TWO MINUTES IS UP.

I'D BE LYING IF I SAID I WASN'T HOPING THIS WAS GONNA HAPPEN.

HEY, COME BACK.
Y'DON'T GET TO WELSH ON ME TWICE.

BRO BRO BRO BRO BRO BRO BRO BRO BRO BRO BRO BRO BRO BRO BRO
SERIOUSLY SERIOUSLY SERIOUSLY SERIOUSLY SERIOUSLY SERIOUSLY
SKREEEE
VROOOOM

BAM!
CRAAAASHH!
Y'STILL OWE ME THAT FIVE DOLLARS, TOO.

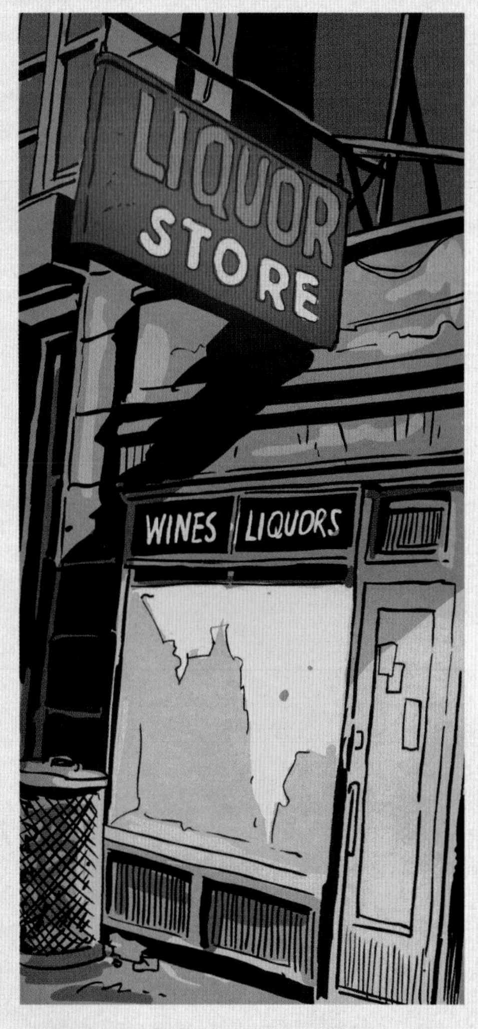
LIQUOR STORE
WINES
LIQUORS

GIVE ME A BOTTLE. OF ANYTHING.
AND A QUARTER TO MAKE A PHONE CALL.

CAN YOU BREAK A HUNDRED?

HEY, GUESS WHAT?
CHICKENBUTT.

DID YOU MEAN NINE IN THE *MORNING* OR NINE AT *NIGHT?*

SAME OL' CLINT, HUH.

"BOYS...

"...THERE'S BEEN A TERRIBLE ACCIDENT. I'M AFRAID YOUR PARENTS ARE DEAD."

BOYS?

CLINT?

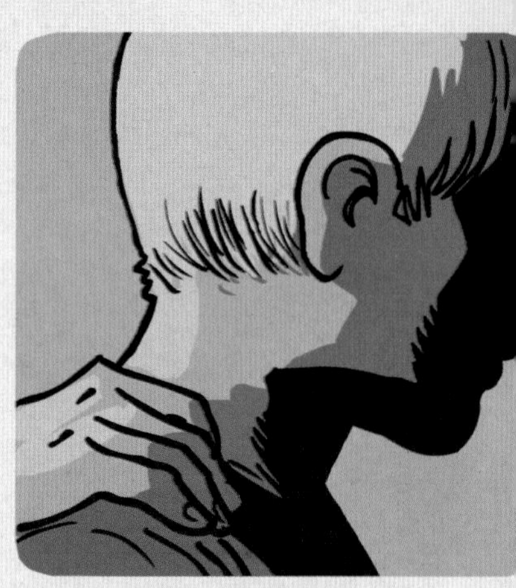

GOOD.

SAME OL' BARNEY, HUH?

C'MERE.

FRACTION + FRANCAVILLA 2013

HAWKEYE ANNUAL #1

I GOTTA GET OUT OF HERE FOR A LITTLE WHILE.
CLINT?
DO WHAT YOU GOTTA DO.
ARE YOU EVEN LISTENING TO ME?
...
I CAN'T STICK AROUND AND WATCH YOU DO THIS TO YOURSELF ANYMORE.
THINGS ARE HARD, THINGS ARE TERRIBLE, YOU STICK TOGETHER.
REAL PEOPLE WOULD STICK TOGETHER. YOU DON'T HOLE UP AND SHUT EVERYBODY OUT.
PLEASE, JUST.
JUST STOP TALKING.
I CAN'T--
--WHERE ARE YOU TAKING MY STUFF?
THIS STUFF IS MY STUFF.
YOU HAD THAT MUCH STUFF OVER HERE?
WHATEVER.

I CAN'T WATCH YOU COMPLETELY LOSE IT ANYMORE, CLINT. I CAN'T JUST SIT HERE AS YOU THROW YOUR LIFE AWAY BECAUSE YOU NEED SOMEONE TO YELL AT AS IT HAPPENS.
YOU MADE A DECISION TO MAKE THIS PLACE YOUR HOME, TO MAKE THESE PEOPLE YOUR FAMILY.

YOU CAN'T JUST BAIL WHEN IT GETS HARD.

WELL, I PUT SOME OF MYYYY ARROWS IN THERE. SOME OF THE WEIRD ONES, SO BE CAREFUL.
A REMOTE EXPLOSIVE ONE. OR TEN. THERE'S A LITTLE KEYFOB-JOBBY THING YOU--
--JUST DON'T BLOW YOUR HEAD OFF OR TRY TAKING IT ON ANY PLANES.
GOT IT, GREAT, GOOD.
GO SCREW.

BUT SERIOUSLY, WHERE ARE YOU GONNA GO?

HEY.
HEY!

YOU'RE NOT MY GIRLFRIEND! YOU CAN'T--
--YOU CAN'T JUST TAKE MY DOG!

SO, WHAT? BACK TO MIDTOWN? BACK TO DADDY'S?

GO TO HELL.

SERIOUSLY, THAT'S MY QUIVER.
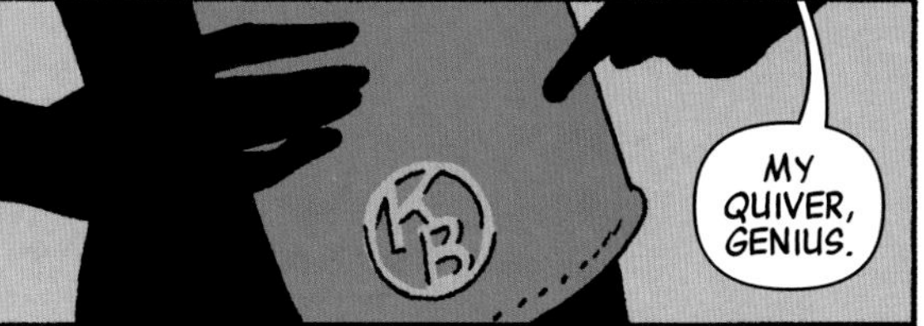
MY QUIVER, GENIUS.

I DON'T KNOW.
LOS ANGELES MAYBE.

GREAT IDEA.
BECAUSE THE WEST COAST TOTALLY NEEDS A HAWKEYE.

C'MON, LUCKY.

WHO THE HELL DO YOU THINK YOU ARE?

WHO IS KATE BISHOP?
IN A WORD... "TROUBLE."
SHE'S BRASH, SHE'S ARROGANT, AND SHE'S YOUNG.
SHE POSSESSES A STRONG DEGREE OF SKILL AND IS A WELL-ABOVE-AVERAGE COMBATANT--SELF-TAUGHT--AND OVERCOMPENSATES FOR LACK OF EXPERIENCE WITH AN UNPREDICTABLE BRAVADO.
SHE'S OPERATED WITH A GROUP IN MANHATTAN ON AND OFF FOR A COUPLE YEARS NOW, AND RECENTLY, WE ARE ALL WELL AWARE, WITH HER NAMESAKE, THE HAWKEYE KNOWN AS CLINT BARTON.
BETTER BE GOING SOMEWHERE WITH THIS, BRANTLEY. I'M IN A MOOD TODAY.
I CAN'T BELIEVE WE LIVE IN WORLD WHERE THERE ARE TWO HAWKEYES TO WORRY ABOUT.

EVER SINCE YOUR UNFORTUNATE ENCOUNTER IN MADRIPOOR, WE'VE BEEN KEEPING AN EYE ON HER, LOOKING FOR THE RIGHT OPPORTUNITY, MA'AM.
WE HAVE REASON TO BELIEVE WE'VE FOUND THAT OPPORTUNITY.
WE HAVE REASON TO BELIEVE SHE'S ON HER WAY TO LOS ANGELES.
AND WE HAVE REASON TO BELIEVE SHE WILL BE ALONE.

WE EVEN HAVE HER CREDIT CARD AND HOME ADDRESS.
DATA MINING IS PULLING EVERYTHING ELSE. SHE'LL BE OURS BY BEDTIME.
BRANTLEY...

WHAT REASON, PRECISELY, DO YOU HAVE TO BELIEVE ALL THIS?

MA'AM...

"...SHE MADE A RESERVATION."
MOMMA LIKE.

MOMMA LIKE A **LOT**.

Okay...

...this looks ***sweet.***

The perfect place to lay low, work on my ever-elusive ***base tan,*** *and drink by a pool.*

Perfect.

NO.
DAD, MY... ***MENTOR...***GUY... AND I JUST KIND OF... BROKE UP? I DON'T NEED ***YOU*** DRAGGING ME INTO ***YOUR*** MIDLIFE CRISIS TOO--
I DON'T WANT HER DAMN DIAZEPAM, AND I DON'T WANT HER SAYING SHE'S MY MOM, OKAY?
IS ***THAT*** WHO MY DAUGHTER IS? SOME ANGRY LITTLE GIRL LASHING OUT AT THE WORLD FOR DARING TO BE A LITTLE HAPPY?

And so, for a whole slate of reasons both professional and personal, our heroine got the "H" out of Dodge.
It wasn't safe, it wasn't fun, and everybody sucks but me.
So I'm gonna go lie low where the suckers can't touch me.
WEST COAST AVENGER
A LADY HAWKEYE EXTRAVAGANZA DELIVERED BY YOURS TRULY:
MATT FRACTION & JAVIER PULIDO
WITH
MATT HOLLINGSWORTH
CLAYTON COWLES
AND
STEPHEN WACKER
TOM BRENNAN

While they try to figure out Dad's credit card sitch, the geniuses at mission control there at least let me wait by the pool.
and they brought me a fruity drink.
Okay, so maybe it's not a **great** way to start things off.
Still, once the guy inside waves his magic fixit wand over my card--
YES SIR, MR. BENTLEY, SIR. DESTROYING IT NOW.
AND YES...
...I'M DISPATCHING MY, AHH--
--AGENTS--
--TO TAKE CARE OF HER TRANSPORTATION. THEY'VE ALREADY DEALT WITH HER **EFFECTS...**
--everything will be a piece of...
...of...

...CRAP.
PARDON ME.
ANY CHANCE YOU COULD HAND ME MY TOWEL?
UH.
YEAH, SURE.
...
ARE YOU...ARE YOU FAMOUS?
YOU LOOK LIKE YOU SHOULD BE FAMOUS.

NO.
I MIGHT AS WELL WEAR A MASK ALL THE TIME FOR ALL ANYBODY KNOWS OF ME.
WHITNEY FROST.

I'M KATE HAWKGUY.
BISHOP.
BISHOP KATE HAWKGUY?
KATE BISHOP!
MMRF?

I'M SORRY. YOU'RE REALLY STRIKING.
AHH-- THANK YOU...?
I SWEAR I'M NOT USUALLY THIS GOON-Y. IT'S BEEN A DAY, AND THE GUYS AT THE FRONT DESK--
LUCKY!

I'M SORRY, I'LL BE RIGHT BACK--
Don't--
IS EVERYTHING ALL RIGHT...?
LUCKY!
--don't embarrass me here, stupid dog--

ARROW!
PIZZA DOG!

HEY!

HEY!
HEY HEY HEY, THAT'S MY CAR!
KATE, WATCH OUT--!
THAT'S MY CAR! HEY! HEY!
TELL IT TO THE REPO COMPANY, HONEY.
JERK!
YOU!
STOP HIM, LUCKY!
KILL HIM--MAUL HIM OR--

HIIYAH!

EEYYOWW!

BOW.
HE GAH MY BOW...
PARDON ME, MISS BISHOP...?

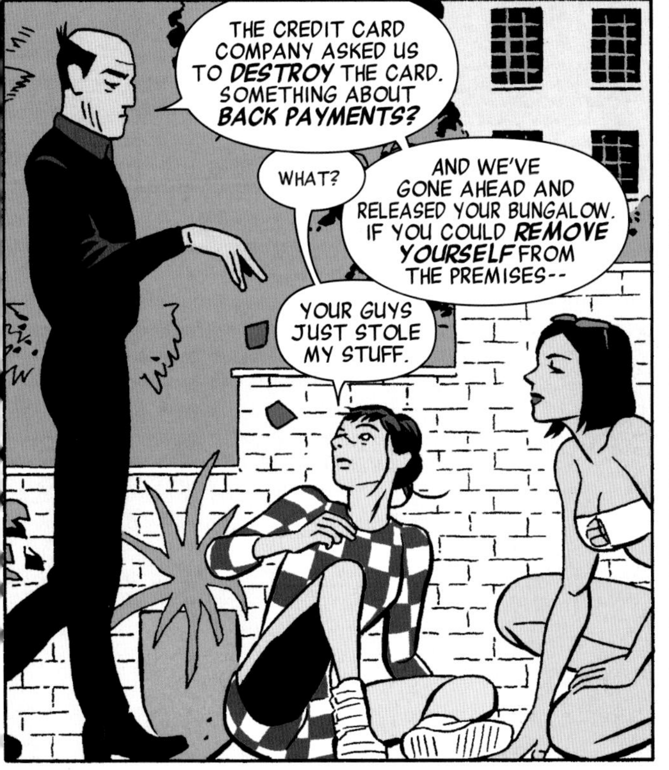
THE CREDIT CARD COMPANY ASKED US TO DESTROY THE CARD. SOMETHING ABOUT BACK PAYMENTS?
WHAT?
AND WE'VE GONE AHEAD AND RELEASED YOUR BUNGALOW. IF YOU COULD REMOVE YOURSELF FROM THE PREMISES--
YOUR GUYS JUST STOLE MY STUFF.

THEY WEREN'T "OUR GUYS."
THEY WERE ALL DRESSED LIKE BELLBOYS.
"BELLMEN."
AND I'M SURE IT'S JUST AN UNFORTUNATE COINCIDENCE.

GANGS THESE DAYS. WHAT CAN YOU DO?
I'VE BEEN IN L.A. JUST TEN MINUTES--
TEN MINUTES.

--HOW DID MY LIFE FALL APART THIS FAST?

I WAS GOING TO GOOGLE YOU WHILE YOU WERE GONE SO WHEN YOU CAME BACK I'D HAVE SOMETHING INTELLIGENT TO TALK ABOUT, BUT...
NO BARS?
NO JUICE. AND THE CORD WAS IN THE CAR...

OPEN
NO PROBLEM.
WHAT WOULD YOU LIKE TO KNOW?
WHO... UH...

WHO ARE YOU, NICE LADY?
WHITNEY FROST. I WAS BORN IN ITALY TO A REAL-LIFE COUNT DRACULA-STYLE COUNT.
HE SPOILED ME ROTTEN AND THEN DROPPED DEAD, LEAVING ME TO TAKE OVER THE FAMILY BUSINESS AND HIS TWO ULCERS.
MY DOCTORS THINK I'LL HAVE A PERMANENT SLEEP DISORDER BY THE TIME I'M 35, SO I GOT THAT GOING FOR ME, WHICH IS NICE.

BECAUSE THE FAMILY BUSINESS IS MURDER.
SO MUCH SO THAT I MAKE MYSELF TAKE THESE LAME OVERNIGHT STAYCATIONS AT A HOTEL THREE MILES FROM MY HOUSE.
OTHERWISE, IT'LL BE THREE ULCERS BY THIRTY-THREE. HELLO.
AND WHY ARE YOU BEING SO NICE TO ME?

BECAUSE YOUR--YOUR LIFE EXPLODED RIGHT IN FRONT OF ME!
I DON'T KNOW. YOU SHARED YOUR TOWEL? HOW COULD I NOT AT LEAST BUY YOU LUNCH?

NOT A FAN OF ASKING FOR HELP, ARE YOU?

I FUTZING HATE IT.

SO YOU HAVE TO DO IT, RIGHT?
IT'S NOTHING. I HAVE SPACE. LET ME PUT YOU UP UNTIL YOU GET IT TOGETHER.
I HAVE...

...LIKE **EIGHTY DOLLARS.** I HAVE ALMOST EIGHTY DOLLARS. PLEASE TAKE IT.
YOU ARE GOING TO NEED THAT EIGHTY DOLLARS TO CLAW YOUR WAY OUT OF THIS GRAVE YOU'VE DUG YOURSELF.
LET ME BE A GOOD DAMN SAMARITAN, OKAY?

OKAY.
YAY! OKAY.
THANK YOU.
PLEASE.

HEY.
YOU'RE A KID. KIDS SMOKE.
DO YOU HAVE ANY CIGARETTES?

SMOKE CIGARETTES. CHILDREN SMOKE CIGARETTES. ARE YOU ONE?

...NO?

SORRY. NEVER PICKED IT UP.
AHH, NEVER CAN TELL. I'M A SOCIAL SMOKER--AND I LIKE BEING SOCIAL TEN, FIFTEEN, TIMES A DAY.
YOU READY TO GO SEE THE HOUSE?

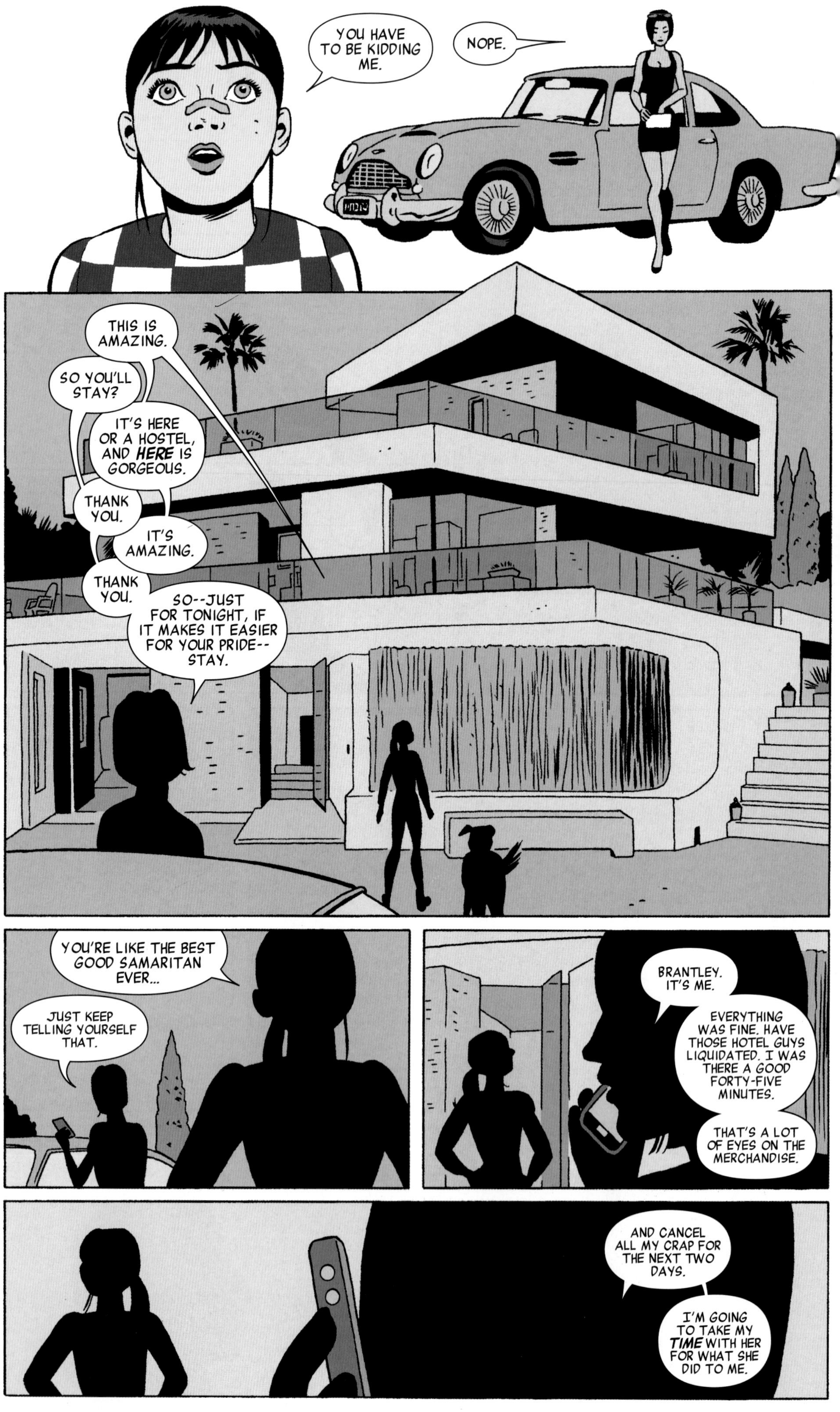

YOU HAVE TO BE KIDDING ME.
NOPE.
THIS IS AMAZING.
SO YOU'LL STAY?
IT'S HERE OR A HOSTEL, AND ***HERE*** IS GORGEOUS.
THANK YOU.
IT'S AMAZING.
THANK YOU.
SO--JUST FOR TONIGHT, IF IT MAKES IT EASIER FOR YOUR PRIDE-- STAY.

YOU'RE LIKE THE BEST GOOD SAMARITAN EVER...
JUST KEEP TELLING YOURSELF THAT.
BRANTLEY. IT'S ME.
EVERYTHING WAS FINE. HAVE THOSE HOTEL GUYS LIQUIDATED. I WAS THERE A GOOD FORTY-FIVE MINUTES.
THAT'S A LOT OF EYES ON THE MERCHANDISE.

AND CANCEL ALL MY CRAP FOR THE NEXT TWO DAYS.
I'M GOING TO TAKE MY ***TIME*** WITH HER FOR WHAT SHE DID TO ME.

SO SHE KNOWS.
BUT--
It's just a phone call away, Darth Kate-r.
BUT WE KNOW.
Call Dad.
RIGHT? RIGHT.
Or call your team.
SO SHE KNOWS--BUT WE KNOW SHE KNOWS.
WHICH SHE DOESN'T KNOW.
All the help you could possibly need is just a futzin' phone call--
AND SHE DOESN'T KNOW SHE DOESN'T KNOW BECAUSE SHE THINKS WE DON'T KNOW.
Don't make it.
WE'RE THE UNKNOWN UNKNOWN!
Let it ride. Play it out some.
=GASP!= LUCKY!--WE'RE A TAUTOLOGY.
You got this.
Can you do this on your own?
I think...
WELL?
THIS ADEQUATE FOR YOUR NEEDS FOR A DAY OR TWO?
I think I want to find out.
COULDN'T BE BETTER.
THIS'LL BE FUN.

KATIE...
DAD...
NO, KATIE, I MEAN IT. WHY WONT YOU COME WITH US? IS IT BECAUSE HEATHER--
DAD--
NO OFFENSE, BUT IT'S LITERALLY GOT NOTHING TO DO WITH HEATHER.
NONE TAKEN.
BUT YOU DON'T WANT ME THERE. YOU WANT ANOTHER DRINK STEWARD. OR A PHOTOGRAPHER. OR SOMEONE TO FIX YOUR SAT-PHONE WHEN IT GIVES YOU TROUBLE WHEN WE HIT THE BOSPORUS AGAIN...
GO WITH HEATHER AROUND THE WORLD ON YOUR BOAT AND BE HAPPY, DADDY.
I'M GONNA GO TRY AND FIGURE OUT HOW TO BE HAPPY WITH ME FOR A LITTLE BIT. STAND ON MY OWN TWO FEET AND SEE WHAT SHAKES, Y'KNOW?
YOU GAVE ME ROOTS AND WINGS, DADDY.
ROOTS AND WINGS. I WON'T LET YOU DOWN.
I PROMISE.
...BUT I PAY ALL YOUR BILLS, KATIE...
"SO YOU'RE NOT ONE OF THOSE SPOILED RICH GIRLS BEING GROOMED TO TAKE OVER THE FAMILY BUSINESS, THEN.
"YOU'VE HAD TO WORK FOR A LIVING."

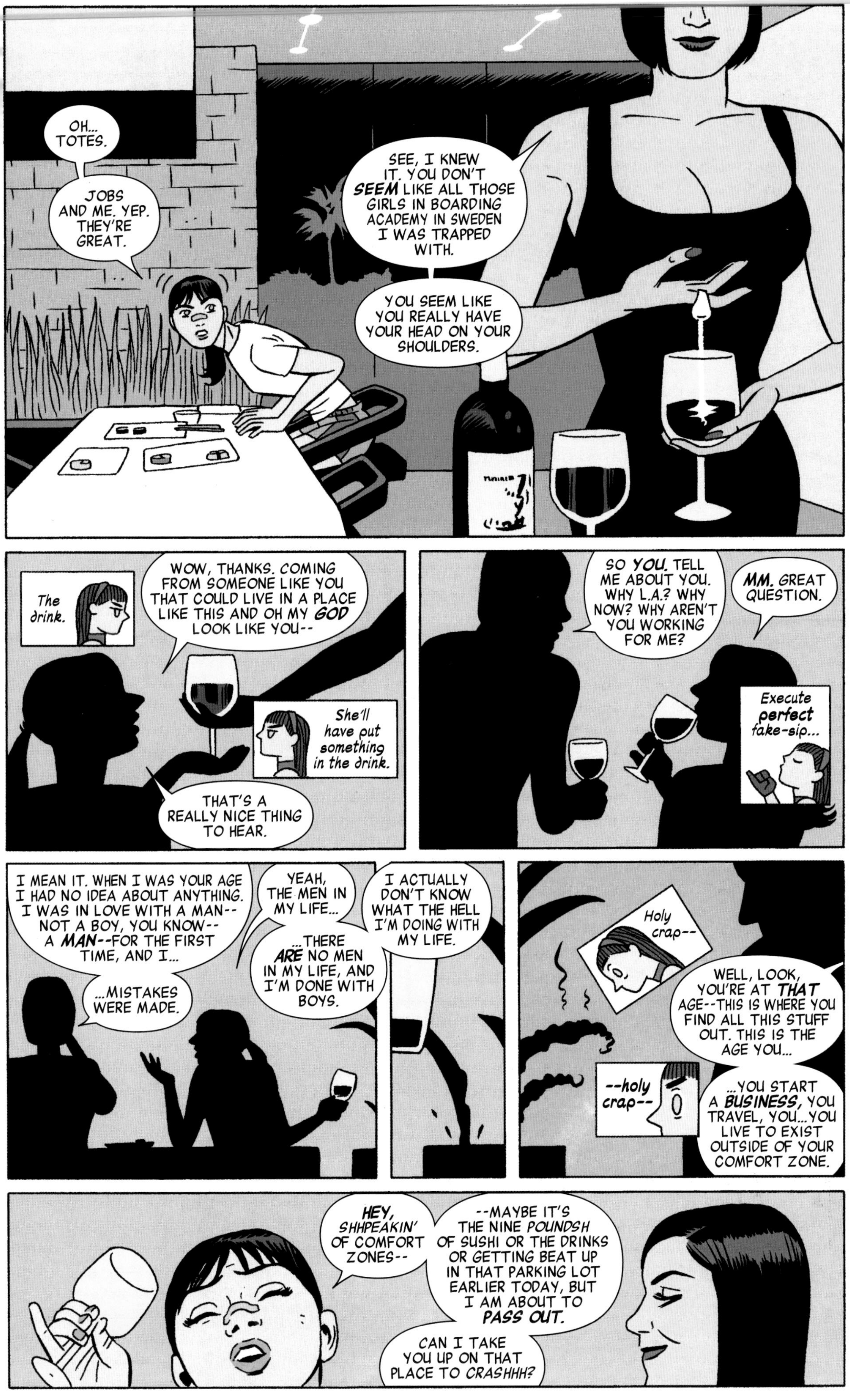

OH... TOTES.

JOBS AND ME. YEP. THEY'RE GREAT.

SEE, I KNEW IT. YOU DON'T ***SEEM*** LIKE ALL THOSE GIRLS IN BOARDING ACADEMY IN SWEDEN I WAS TRAPPED WITH.

YOU SEEM LIKE YOU REALLY HAVE YOUR HEAD ON YOUR SHOULDERS.

HEY, SHHPEAKIN' OF COMFORT ZONES--

--MAYBE IT'S THE NINE *POUNDSH* OF SUSHI OR THE DRINKS OR GETTING BEAT UP IN THAT PARKING LOT EARLIER TODAY, BUT I AM ABOUT TO ***PASS OUT.***

SLEEP TIGHT.
SEE YOU REAL SOON.
ZZRRRRKKK
Wait for it...
Wait for iiittt...
C'MON, BOY.
Okay, **this...**
OH, BOY.
...this looks bad.
Is there a plan here, Kate?
Do we have a plan?
Totes have a plan. The plan is--
Okay, so. So...
So she's **Madame Masque,** right?
Yes. But we can't prove it.
Evidence! We need evidence.
Just because she... what, said something **Masque** said she's--
--what **exactly** would be evidence?
Well, her mask, I guess.
She drugged your drink, she said the thing,
Oh, dude, I bet she's behind all of this crazy-- **everything** since you first got here--
--what if she's just a helpful weirdo who--
--how about you just get the hell out of her house before she tries to kill you, Kate?

LUCKY.
GET IN THE CAR.

SKREECH
WELL, I DON'T KNOW HOW, BUT YOU'RE PAYING FOR THAT.
AAAIIIEE!

CAN YOU APPRECIATE HOW... COSMICALLY ORDAINED THIS REVENGE IS? HOW MUCH I'VE WANTED PAYBACK FOR WHAT YOU DID TO ME IN MADRIPOOR?
I NEVER UNDERSTOOD WHY YOU DIDN'T TAKE MY MASK OFF WHEN YOU HAD THE CHANCE. JUST THINK-- YOU COULD'VE AVOIDED ALL OF THIS IF YOU'D ONLY PEEKED.
THAT'S THE DIFFERENCE BETWEEN YOU AND ME.
I RESPECT BOUNDARIES.

IS YOUR NAME REALLY WHITNEY FROST?

UNBELIEVABLE.
GET HER OUT OF THE CAR.

LUCKY.
DOWN.

SKREECH
VRROOM

POP!

DAMMIT, LOOK AT WHAT SHE DID TO MY DECOYS...

WHERE YOU WANT HER, MA'AM?

TO THE PAIN ROOM, WHERE DO YOU THINK?

I SWEAR YOU'RE ALL USELESS--

MUH.

MY STUFF. 'ZAT MY STUFF?

YOU'VE CRASHED YOUR PRECIOUS "STUFF" ALL OVER MY WORK FACILITY.

AND BOUGHT YOURSELF ANOTHER DAY IN THE PAIN ROOM BEFORE I LET YOU DIE.

I ASSURE YOU THE BUMS DOWN ON SUNSET WILL BE WEARING ALL YOUR "STUFF" BY SUNRISE TOMORROW.

EXPLODING ARROW OR TEN.

KEY-FOB JOBBY.

SUCK IT, SUPER-BITCH.

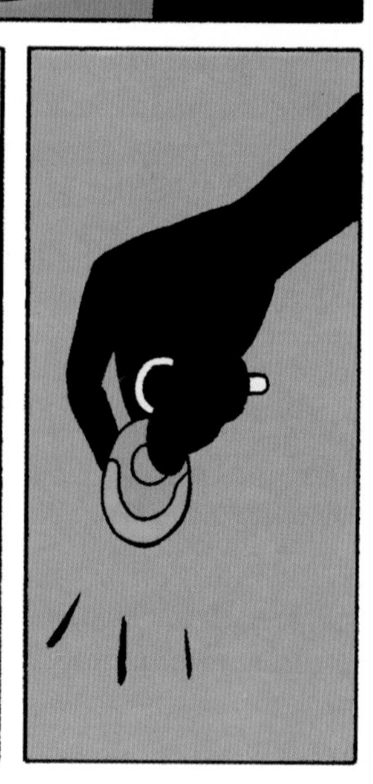

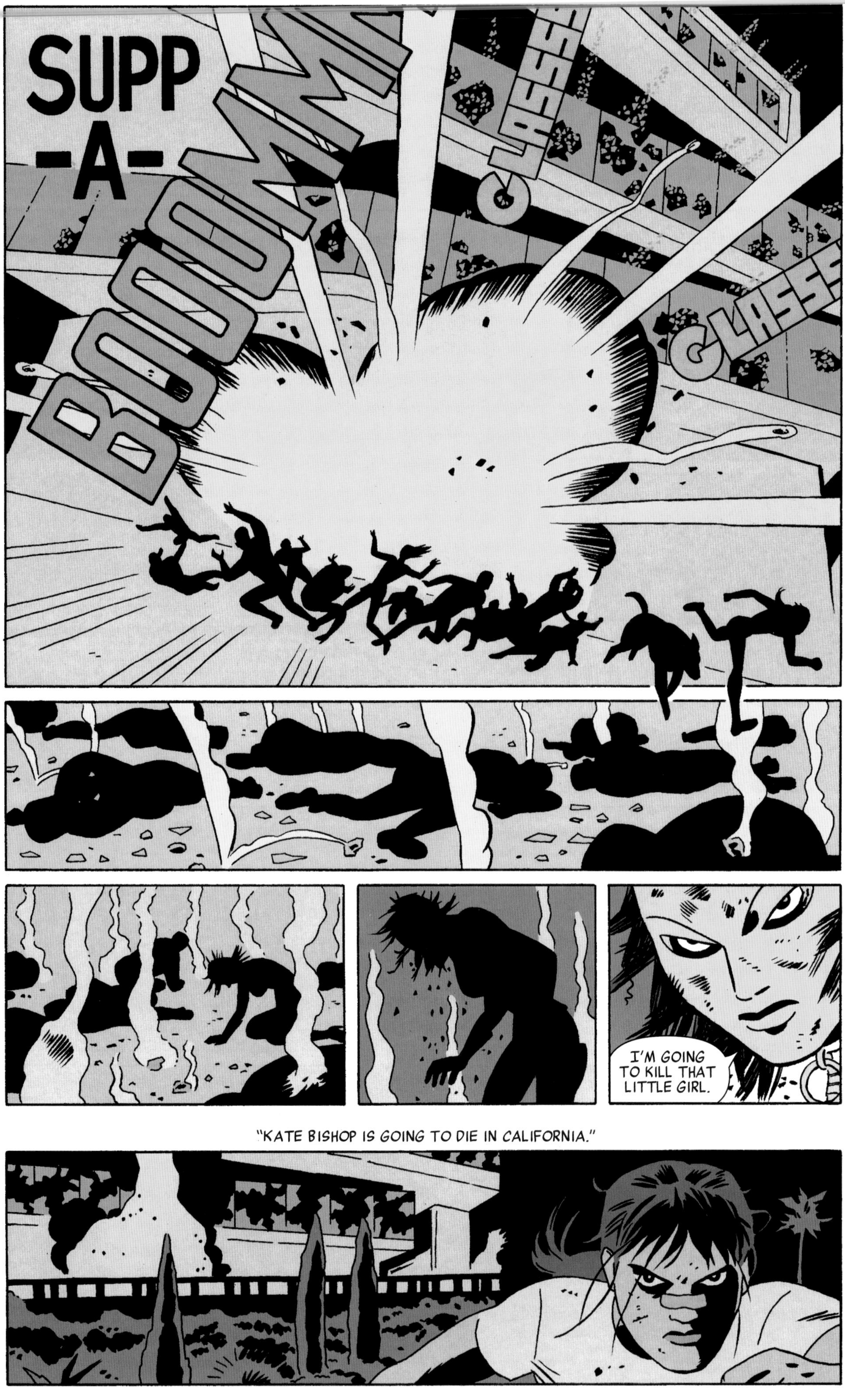

SUPP
-A-
BOOOM!

GLASS

"KATE BISHOP IS GOING TO DIE IN CALIFORNIA."

LOOK: I'VE NEVER HAD A JOB. NOT A REAL JOB. NOT A JOB MY DAD DIDN'T GET ME.
BUT I'VE WORKED. I'VE WORKED HARD FOR THINGS.
HARDER THAN YOU'D EVER BELIEVE.
NOT THAT YOU HAVE TO! I'M JUST SAYING.
BUT I NEVER NEEDED A JOB BECAUSE I NEVER NEEDED MONEY UNTIL NOW.
LOOK, WE'RE ALL ADULTS HERE; WE'VE ALL SEEN THE "WELCOME TO THE JUNGLE" VIDEO.
I COWBOYED OUT TO LOS ANGELES AND IN THE SPAN OF FORTY-EIGHT HOURS GOT TAKEN FOR EVERYTHING I HAD. IT'S AN OLD STORY, AND MAYBE I SHOULD'VE KNOWN BETTER.
ROOKIE MISTAKE, RIGHT?
BUT I AM TELLING YOU NOW: I MIGHT BE *YOUNG*, BUT I AM *GOOD*. I WORK *HARD*, AND I'M A GOOD PERSON.
I KNOW WHAT'S RIGHT. I KNOW WHAT'S WRONG. AND IF YOU GIVE ME THIS CHANCE--
IF YOU JUST GIVE ME ONE *SHOT* TO SHOW YOU HOW GOOD I CAN BE, HOW HARD I WORK, HOW *MUCH* I BELIEVE IN DOING THE RIGHT THING--
--I WON'T LET YOU DOWN.
WHOA. THAT WAS, LIKE, SURPRISINGLY INTENSE...
...HE ONLY, LIKE, EATS THIS ONE KIND OF SPECIAL BRAND AND--
...YEAH, MAN, REALLY WE JUST NEED SOMEONE TO HOUSESIT OUR TRAILER ON THE BEACH AND, LIKE, FEED OUR MR. STARSHADOWS, OUR *CAT*...
LADIES, I CAN DO THIS.

YOU HAVE REALLY GREAT ENERGY.
I THINK WE FOUND OUR SUPER HERO.
THE FESTIVAL STARTS IN A COUPLE DAYS--HOW SOON COULD YOU START?

COULD YOU DRIVE ME TO THE NEAREST SPORTING GOODS STORE?

SPORTING GOODS
...OKAY, THAT'S A BEGINNER'S RECURVE BOW AND A BUNDLE OF ONE HUNDRED ARROWS AND A JUNIOR MISS QUIVER SET...
THAT COMES TO $282.35 TODAY.

I HAVE... ALMOST SIXTY DOLLARS. FIFTY-EIGHT SOMETHING.
I-I'M SORRY? I DON'T UNDERSTAND.

LOOK: I'VE NEVER HAD A JOB. NOT A REAL JOB.
NOT A JOB MY DAD DIDN'T GET ME...

--But I've worked. I've worked hard for things.
Harder than you'd ever believe.
But I never needed a job because I never needed money until now.
Look, we're all adults here; we've all seen the 'Welcome to the Jungle' video.
I cowboyed out to Los Angeles and in the span of forty-eight hours got taken for everything I had. It's an old story, and maybe I should've known better.
Rookie mistake, right?
But I am telling you now: I might be young, but I am good. I work hard, and I'm a good person.
I know what's right. I know what's wrong. And if you give me this chance--
If you just give me one shot to show you how good I can be, how hard I work, how much I believe in doing the right thing--
--I won't let you down.
I promise.
END

13

HEY, IT'S ME.
UHH--

I GOT A SPELLING...
HOW DO YOU SPELL "INCORRIGIBLE"?

CALL ME BACK?

I, UH. I DON'T HAVE A DICTIONARY. OR INTERNET.

OR, UH.
MUCH OF ANYTHING.
CLICK
BZZZ
BZZZ

BZZZZ*
AVENGERS

YOU OKAY?

YEAH.
OR AT LEAST I CAN GET THERE.

YOU?

YEAH.

...JESS?

I'M *FINE*, CLINT.

I'M FINE.

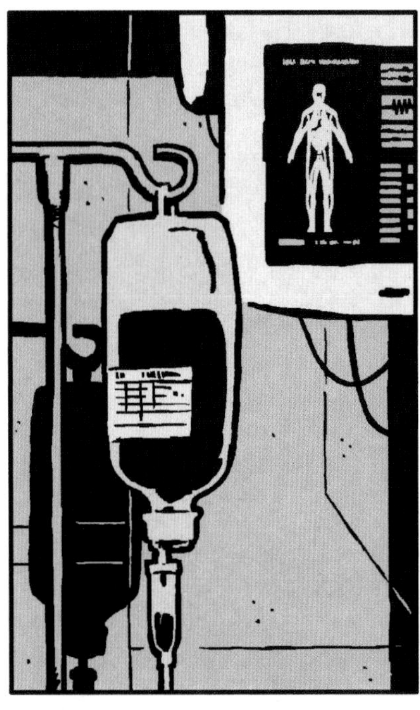

...

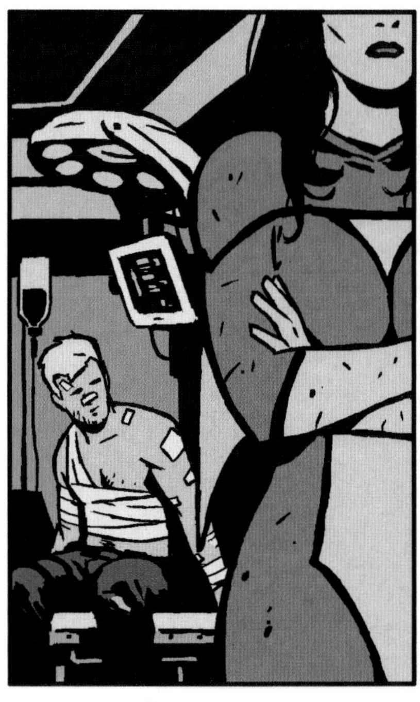

JE--

--BARTON!
IT'S YOUR SIDEKICK.
I DON'T HAVE A SIDE--

BISHOP, DUMMY. WHAT ARE YOU, CONCUSSED?
...ACTUALLY--
--PHONE.

HEY.
...

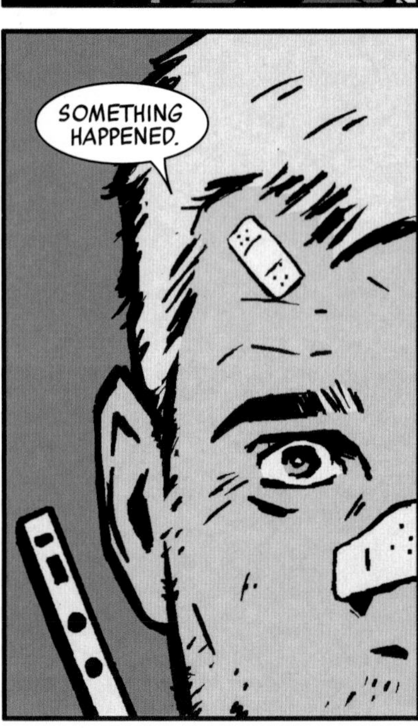
SOMETHING HAPPENED.

a
Clint Barton
- Hawkeye -
Comic Book

by
Matt Fraction
&
David Aja

with
Matt Hollingsworth
&
Chris Eliopoulos

...WHAT DO THEY THINK I'M GOING TO DO?

YOU KNOW WHAT I'M GOING TO DO--

--I'M GOING TO START BLASTING.

WHERE'D YOU GET THAT HAT?

THEY GOT US. WE'RE LICKED.

TOOK YA TWO!

(MUSIC NOTES)

RNNGGG
RNNGGG

RNNGGG
AWWW, PHONE--

RNNGGG

RNNGGG

RNNGGG
I HATE YOU.

...
=SIGH= WHAT?
HA HAHH... HEYYYY, BARN. WHEN DID--AHH--

--WHEN DID YOU GET BACK INTO TOWN?
AHH...YEAH, MAN, SURE, YEAH. I MEAN--
OF COURSE. HOW MUCH DO YOU NEED? WELL, I GOT--
SEE, I GOT A... GUY IN MY BUILDING DIED, THERE'S COPS, I GOTTA TALK TO HIS DAMN DAD--

YEAH, NINE. OKAY. TOMORROW...YEAH, NINE, TEN. LATE.
LET ME GET ALL MY STUFF TAKEN CARE OF AND STUFF.
OKAY?

CLICK

BARNEY FUTZING BARTON.

NOK
NOK
CLINT BARTON?

CLINT BARTON?

HANG ON, HANG ON--
--FINGERS NOT WORKIN' TOO WELL--

ARE YOU THE OWNER AND SUPERINTENDENT OF THIS BUILDING, SIR?

ACTING, UH--
--ACTING...INTERIM... SUPERINTENDENT AND OWNERSHIP... CANDIDATE?
I'M TAKING CARE OF THE PLACE. C'MON IN, BOYS.

HEY, ARE YOU--
NOPE. I'M NOBODY.

CAN WE GET TO THE REAL QUESTIONS HERE, GUYS?
CAN YOU TELL ME WHO KILLED MY NEIGHBOR OR WHAT?

WE WERE HOPING YOU COULD HELP US OUT WITH THAT SOME.
LOOKS LIKE YOUR NEIGHBOR CAUGHT A PROWLER, OR A PROWLER CAUGHT YOUR NEIGHBOR, AT LEAST. WHICH IS WEIRD, BECAUSE, Y'KNOW.

WHY WOULD ANYBODY PROWL A BUILDING LIKE *THIS?* UNLESS THERE'S ANOTHER REASON FOR VIOLENT PEOPLE WITH GUNS TO SNOOP AROUND.
WHAT WERE YOU DOING BEFORE BEING PAGED TO REPORT TO AVENGERS TOWER, MR. BARTON?
OR DO WE GIVE YOU A LITTLE MORE TIME TO WAKE UP BEFORE GETTING TO THE REAL QUESTIONS?

I WAS HERE WRITING UNTIL...
11? 10? SOMEWHERE AROUND THERE, I THINK.

PAGER'S HERE SOMEWHERE, YOU CAN CHECK. I HAD A FEW AND WASN'T PAYING TOO MUCH ATTENTION, TELL YOU THE TRUTH.
CAN ANYBODY CORROBORATE THAT?

I CALLED MY EX-WIFE AT SOME POINT IN THERE.
EX-WIFE?

YEAH, UH. SHE'S--SHE'S AN AVENGER TOO?
I HAD A SPELLING QUESTION.
A SPELLING QUESTION?

LIKE I SAID, I HAD A FEW.

THINK WE'RE DONE HERE.
IF ANYTHING COMES UP YOU GUYS ARE MY FIRST CALL.

THANK YOU, SIR. STAY OUT OF TROUBLE.

NOT MY STRONG SUIT.

GOOD BOY.

DEAD
END

DEMAND THE SAND
REPAIR OUR BEACH
WHAT ABOUT ROCKAWAY BEACH

I just didn't want him to hear about it on the phone, is all.
I didn't want him to be alone.

STARK ALWAYS LOOKS ALL SHARP AND NEAT BUT I PUT ON A SHIRT WITH BUTTONS AND I LOOK LIKE THAT GUY IN THAT MOVIE WHERE HE DIES IN THE END.

COLLAR STAYS.
WHAT?

I PUT IN COLLAR STAYS.
WHAT?

YOU KNOW HOW THE TIPS ALWAYS CURL UP? YOU PUT THESE LITTLE GUYS IN THERE.

"COLLAR STAYS."

YES. AND YOUR COLLAR STAYS IN PLACE.

GREAT. NOW I GOT ANOTHER THING TO WORRY ABOUT I NEVER WORRIED ABOUT BEFORE.

JUST ONCE--ONCE--I'D LIKE TO GET OUT OF HERE WITHOUT YOU BEING A TOTAL ASS, CLINT.

KATE--

BEEEP BEEEPBEEEP
HONNNNK
CLINT?

WHAT, KATE?
I...
GOD, I DON'T EVEN KNOW WHERE TO START.

I'M HERE.
I'M HERE FOR YOU, OKAY?
NO MATTER WHAT.

YOU CAN SCREAM AND YOU CAN YELL AND BE AS MEAN AND SELF-DESTRUCTIVE AS YOU WANT.
BECAUSE I KNOW YOU'RE GOING TO BE HERE FOR ME WHEN IT'S MY TURN TO FALL APART.

LET THEM ALL COME, CLINT.
LET EVERY LAST ONE OF THOSE TRACKSUIT-WEARING SUB-VERBAL BULLYING MURDEROUS SCUMBAGS COME AT US.

BECAUSE YOU AND ME? TOGETHER?
TOGETHER, CLINT, I THINK YOU AND ME ARE THE PERSON WE BOTH WISH WE COULD BE. AND I KNOW *THAT* PERSON...
I KNOW THAT PERSON IS WORTH SOMETHING. I KNOW *THAT* PERSON CAN...CAN PRETTY MUCH DO ANYTHING.

YOU WITH ME, PARTNER?

ZZZZZ SSSANDWICHES ZZZZ.

SANDY
Dumb name for a hurricane

I had a TEACHER named Sandy can't stop thinking about her

Everybody thinking her last name was a cuss word and nobody sayin' it

Wait

Grills?

YEAH DOWN HERE HAWKGUY.

WE'RE ALL DOWN HERE.
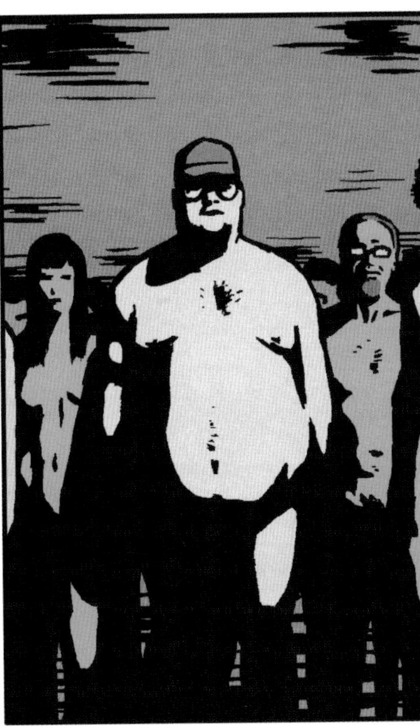

WE'RE HERE CLINT.

IS STUPID, BRO.

SHH.

WHAT STUPID?

"BRO--HE COULD KILL RIGHT NOW.

"HE COULD JUST--"

POW POW POW.

"SERIOUSLY, BRO?"

SHUT UP. BOTH OF YOU.

"KAZIU KNOWS WHAT HE'S DOING."

"HOW HE DOES IT IS FOR HIM.
"BRO."

Barney.
Barney, Barney, Barney.

Same old Barney.

Half an hour waiting around. I'm done.

Good night, Barney Futzing Barton wherever you--

RNNGGG

RNNGGG
AHH, DAMMIT.
WHAT NOW.

RNNGGG

I'M GOING TO MURDER YOU.
=SIGH= WHAT.

NIGHT, DUMMY, I MEANT THAT NIGHT. I ALWAYS MEAN NIGHT.
"UNTIL THE NIGHT WE--"
YEAH, OKAY.

CLICK

BITE MY NECK, LUCK. JUST--JUST CHOMP DOWN ON IT AS HARD AS YOU CAN. OKAY?

HEY.

SPARE THE PRICE OF A CUPPA COFFEE FOR A FELLOW AMERICAN DOWN ON HIS LUCK?

SAME OL' BARNEY, HUH?

C'MERE.

I'M DEAD ON MY FEET, MAN.

COME IN IF YOU'RE COMIN'.
EVERYTHING'S LOCKED UP SAFE AND SOUND.

BUT SERIOUSLY, WHERE ARE YOU GONNA GO?

I DON'T KNOW.
LOS ANGELES MAYBE.

GREAT IDEA.
BECAUSE THE WEST COAST TOTALLY NEEDS A HAWKEYE.
C'MON, LUCKY.

FLUSSSSSH

HEY.
HEY!

HEY.

SHE TOOK MY DOG, MAN.

DUNNO.
LOOKS LIKE THE DOG LEFT, T'ME.

SOMETIMES THEY JUST HAVE A MIND OF THEIR OWN--
--OOPS!

THAT'S OKAY.
THEY LOOK PERFECT.

NG COLD.
BELIEVE IT.
SAID THE SHORE STILL ISN'T BACK.
AND NOW THE FIRES--

...THREATENED TO KILL ME--OR BOBBI--I DUNNO, YOU THREATENED TO KILL SOMEBODY--
--AW BOO HOO, Y'BABY. I THREATENED TO KILL A BACKPACK JUST A SECOND AGO--

HEY, BOSS. WHO'S THIS?

DEKE, EVERYBODY, THIS IS MY BROTHER BARNEY.

HE'S GONNA STICK AROUND. HELP US OUT.

HUNGRY?

I DON'T...
THANKS.

WELCOME TO THE FAMILY.

UHH.
SURE THING.

14

AND HAWKEYE LIVED HAPPILY EVER AFTER.

SERIOUSLY--IT'S NOT SO BAD OUT HERE ON THE EDGE OF PARADISE. I HAVE MY LITTLE ROUTINES...
FRRF.

...I WATCH MY STORIES, DO MY DAILY CHORES AND ERRANDS...
"...AND A SPLASH OF GUAVA MAKES EVERY MOIST MORSEL FELINE-ONIOUSLY DELECT
GIVE ME A BREAK.

ALL IN ALL IT'S BEEN A BLISSFUL, CENTERING, CALMING AND BEAUTIFUL--
EIGHTY-SEVEN DOLLARS AND NINEY-FIVE CENTS. CASH, CREDIT, OR DEBIT?
6
4
5

FOUR DOLLARS, SEVENTEEN CENTS.
NAILED IT.
OH, AND I'M SUPER-BROKE.

LUCKY, WE NEED TO GET A J-O-B.

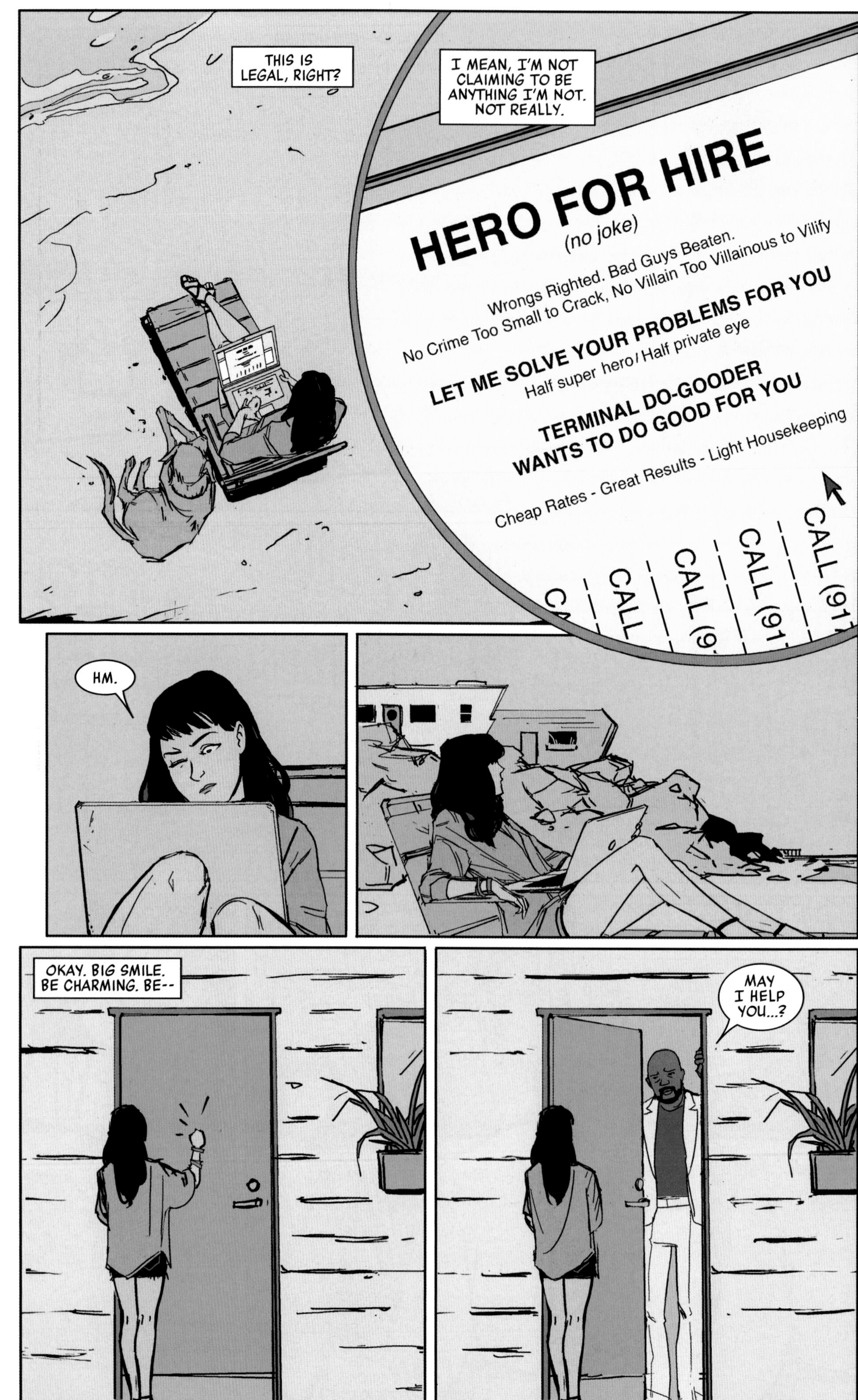
THIS IS LEGAL, RIGHT?
I MEAN, I'M NOT CLAIMING TO BE ANYTHING I'M NOT. NOT REALLY.
HERO FOR HIRE
(no joke)
Wrongs Righted. Bad Guys Beaten.
No Crime Too Small to Crack, No Villain Too Villainous to Vilify
LET ME SOLVE YOUR PROBLEMS FOR YOU
Half super hero/ Half private eye
TERMINAL DO-GOODER WANTS TO DO GOOD FOR YOU
Cheap Rates - Great Results - Light Housekeeping
HM.
OKAY. BIG SMILE. BE CHARMING. BE--
MAY I HELP YOU...?

HI! I'M YOUR--
I'M KATE?
DO YOU HAVE A PRINTER I COULD BORROW BY ANY CHANCE? MINE IS, UH.
IN NEW YORK.

I'LL BE SUPERFAST--
--I-- UH--
--COME IN?
YOU'RE SURE? I MEAN--
HOW IS THAT POSSIBLE?

WHO WOULD STEAL MY ORCHIDS?
BUT IF YOU DON'T GET THE ORCHIDS BACK MY WEDDING WILL BE RUINED--
--BECAUSE I HAD A VISION!

OH, DEAR.
HEY, HE SOUNDS SUPER-BUMMED.
HE IS.
DO YOU LIKE HELVETICA?
I DO.
MY FLYER RULES.
NOW WHAT'S ALL THIS ABOUT SOMEBODY STEALING SOMETHING AND RUINING YOUR BIG DAY?

KATE BISHOP. I'M PRETTY MUCH AN AVENGER.
AT YOUR SERVICE.

IS..."SKINNY WHITE GIRL" AN AVENGER NOW?
MARCUS, BE NICE.
I'M FINCH. AND WE'RE HAVING A BAD DAY, NEIGHBOR.

OKAY, LOOK. MY NAME IS KATE BISHOP, AND I USED TO BE HAWKEYE AND I GUESS I STILL AM BUT I'M KIND OF ON THIS WHOLE SUMMER VOYAGE OF DISCOVERY--
LOOK, I BET I CAN GET YOUR ORCHIDS BACK FOR YOU, DO A LITTLE GOOD, MAYBE YOU PAY ME A MODEST LITTLE BIT OF SCRATCH AND BOOM!
WEDDING SAVED.
I AM A GENIUS.

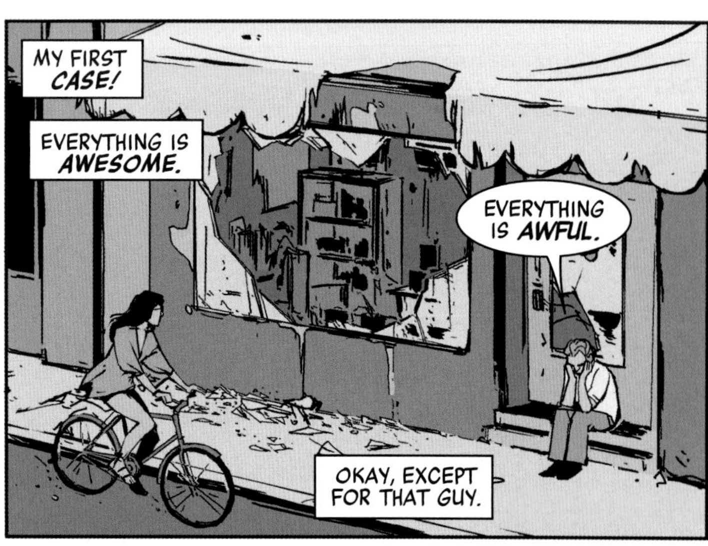
MY FIRST CASE!
EVERYTHING IS AWESOME.
EVERYTHING IS AWFUL.
OKAY, EXCEPT FOR THAT GUY.

WAS THIS YOUR PLACE?
MY PLACE? IT WAS MY LIFE, AND NOW IT'S RUINED.

THAT BASTARD.
THAT BASTARD STOLE MY FLOWERS AND BURNED DOWN MY LIFE.
PLAY IT COOL.
WHICH BASTARD WOULD THAT BE, SIR?

AND HOW CAN YOU TELL HE STOLE SOMETHING FIRST?
IT JUST LOOKS LIKE A BUNCH OF BURN-Y, SMOLDER-Y, STUFF TO ME.
HE TOOK ORCHIDS. I KNOW A GUY WHO KNOWS A GUY--

"THEY WERE FOR A CLIENT. FOR A WEDDING.
"MY CLIENT HAD A VISION, SEE.
"THESE GUYS ARE FRIENDS OF MINE AND THEY WAITED A LONG TIME FOR THIS TO HAPPEN."

I WANTED THEM TO HAVE SOMETHING AS BEAUTIFUL, RARE, AND PATIENT AS THEY WERE. I WANTED THESE ORCHIDS BECAUSE--
GOD, GUYS, I'M SO SORRY.

MISTER FLYNT WARD WAS THE BASTARD'S NAME.

AND WHEN I SAID NO HE GOT VIOLENT.
THEN HE MADE ME WATCH.

SO DID YOU CALL THE COPS? ARE THEY ARRESTING THE GUY? ARE YOU GONNA GET YOUR ORCHIDS BACK?

WHAT ARE YOU, NEW IN TOWN? I CALL THE COPS AND I'M GONNA GET MURDERED.
DON'T YOU KNOW ABOUT FLYNT WARD?

WHO IS FLYNT WARD?

ARE YOU DETECTIVE CAUDLE...? I'M INVESTIGATING THE BURNING OF SHORESIDE FLORAL AND I HAVE QUESTIONS ABOUT FLYNT WARD.
WHO THE HELL ARE--
I DON'T--
WHAT THE HELL?

KATE BISHOP. SHORESIDE FLORAL WAS--
THAT WAS THE PLACE OVER OFF OCEAN?
THE INVESTIGATION IS ONGOING.
SHAKE

ARE YOU-- DO YOU HAVE ANY LEADS?

WELL...THE BURN LINES LOOKED LIKE A TETRIS GAME SO WE'RE PRETTY SURE IT'S ARSON.
WHY? DO YOU HAVE A LEAD FOR US?
AND WHO THE HELL ARE YOU?

KATE BISHOP.
THE HELL IS THAT TO ME?
IT MEANS I'M GONNA CRACK THIS CASE.
WHAT DO YOU--
THE FLORIST TOLD ME A GUY NAMED FLYNT WARD DID IT.
DID YOU JUST WINK AT ME?
YEP! BECAUSE THANKS TO THIS FLORIST OF MINE I'M GONNA CRACK THIS CASE.

HE WANT TO PRESS CHARGES, THIS FLORIST OF YOURS?

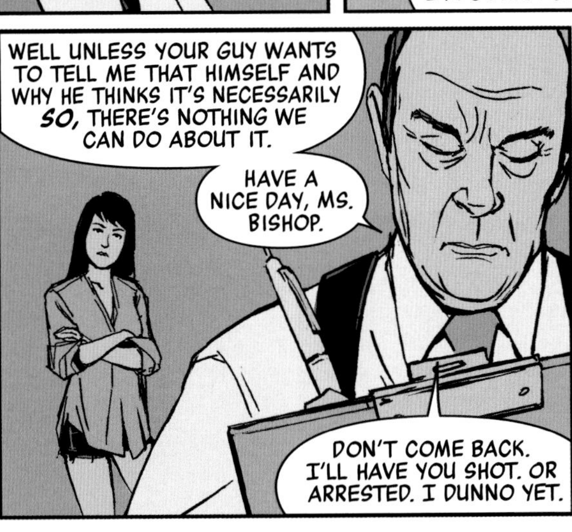
WELL UNLESS YOUR GUY WANTS TO TELL ME THAT HIMSELF AND WHY HE THINKS IT'S NECESSARILY SO, THERE'S NOTHING WE CAN DO ABOUT IT.
HAVE A NICE DAY, MS. BISHOP.
DON'T COME BACK. I'LL HAVE YOU SHOT. OR ARRESTED. I DUNNO YET.

GENTLEMEN, I GOT IT ALL FIGURED OUT.

SOME GUY TRIED TO BUY YOUR SPECIAL FLOWERS BUT YOUR GUY, HE WOULDN'T SELL.
THEN THE FIRST GUY, WHO'S A GUY CALLED FLYNT WARD BY THE BY, BEAT HIM UP.
THEN HE STOLE THE FLOWERS AND BURNED YOUR GUY'S STORE DOWN.
AND HE IS A SCARY GUY BECAUSE YOUR GUY, FLOWER GUY, DOESN'T WANT TO GO TO THE COPS.
OH, WAIT.
I BET YOU ALREADY KNOW ALL THAT.

ANYWAY I'M GONNA GO CHECK OUT MR. FLYNT WARD AND SEE WHAT SHAKES.

WE DON'T WANT ANY TROUBLE.
WE JUST WANT OUR FLOWERS BACK. IT SEEMS SILLY BUT A VISION IS A VISION AND A DREAM IS A--
--WE WAITED A LONG TIME FOR THIS.

IF I TAKE THIS CASE... IF I RETRIEVE THESE ORCHIDS FOR YOU... CAN YOU PAY ME? I HATE TO ASK BUT I GOT THIS CAT, HE ONLY EATS THIS ONE KIND OF CAT FOOD...

"CASE"--? "TAKE" THIS "CASE"--?
I'M SORRY, ARE YOU--
ARE YOU A PRIVATE DETECTIVE, OR...

EVEN BETTER.
I'M A SUPER HERO.

arson
evidence
private detective
arson law
how to be a private detective in california
aljdf:lkjlkj
CLIK.
HEY!
YOU!
UH-- OFFICER!
COP!
DETECTIVE COP MAN!
"CAUDLE."
YES! THAT. YES.
NICE WORKING WITH YOU TODAY.
WHO ARE YOU AGAIN?
ARSON CASE. ANNOYING GIRL. FLYNT WARD.
HOW CAN I GET YOU TO ARREST FLYNT WARD? WHY AREN'T YOU DOING ANYTH--
YOU ARE MEDDLING IN AN ONGOING INVESTIGATION, KID! DON'T YOU GET IT?
THERE ARE REAL PEOPLE-- ACTUAL PROFESSIONAL ADULTS-- TRAINED IN THE LAW AND HOW TO ENFORCE THOSE LAWS.
WE'RE THE GOOD GUYS AND IF YOU REALLY CARE ABOUT GETTING THE BAD GUYS HERE--
YOU'LL KNOCK IT OFF, MISS BISHOP.
OR I WILL ARREST YOU.
NOT IF I ARREST YOU FIRST.
ZING.
NO, WAIT, THAT ZING SUCKED.
AND I DON'T LIKE STUFF THAT SUCKS.

ARRRGH!
HOW CAN THEY BE OUT?!

RRRRR--

CATS, HUH? PAIN IN THE ASS.
Y'KNOW I BEEN SHOPPING HERE A *LONNNG* TIME...

...AND YOU KINDA LEARN AFTER A WHILE THAT IF YOU DON'T GIVE UP...

...YOU CAN FIND WHAT YOU NEED.

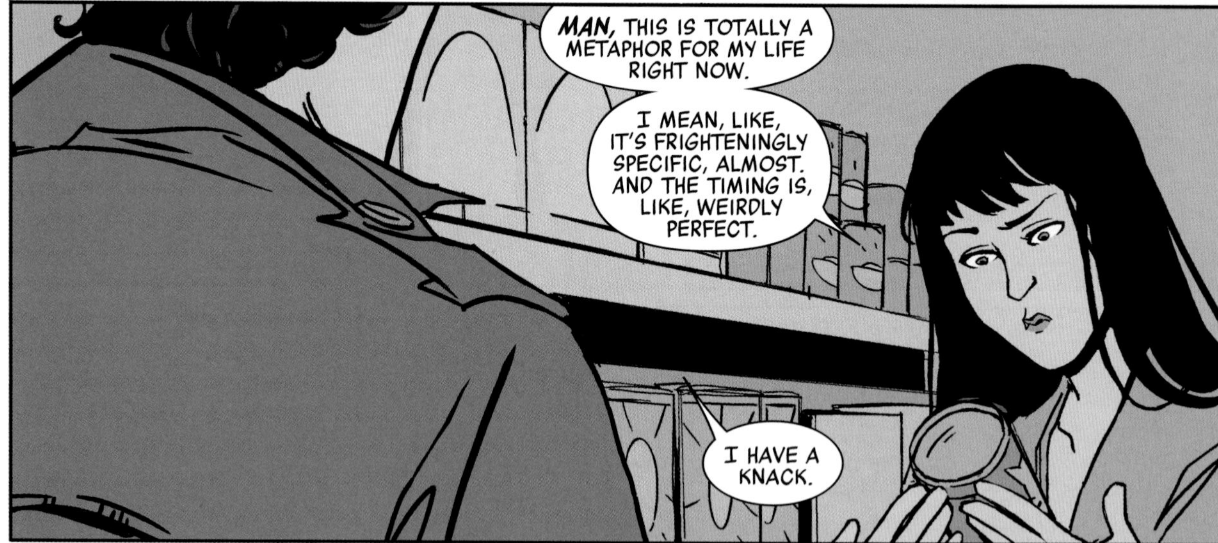
MAN, THIS IS TOTALLY A METAPHOR FOR MY LIFE RIGHT NOW.
I MEAN, LIKE, IT'S FRIGHTENINGLY SPECIFIC, ALMOST. AND THE TIMING IS, LIKE, WEIRDLY PERFECT.
I HAVE A KNACK.

IT'S OKAY IF I BUY THIS ONE?
IT'S OKAY BY ME.
MINE IS A BLUE-LABEL PAIN-IN-THE-ASS.
SEE YA 'ROUND, KID.
AND NEVER STOP LOOKING.

PLAN A.
PLAY IT COOL, KATE-SILVER-OF-THE-FIVE-THIRTY-KATE-BLOG.

JUST WALK UP THERE CALM AND CASUAL, KNOCK ON THE DOOR AND SAY--

ORCHIDS.

ARE YOU FLYNT WARD? I UNDERSTAND YOU'RE THE MAN A WOMAN MUST SEE IF SHE'S IN THE MARKET FOR CERTAIN...
"ORCHIDS."

I...I BEG YOUR PARDON?

ORCHIDS, WARD, I'M LOOKING TO BUY SOME ORCHIDS AND WAS TOLD BY EVERYBODY WHO'S POSITIVELY ANYBODY THAT THE ONLY BODY ANY ONE MUST SPEAK WITH REGARDING SUCH THINGS IS YOU, WARD COMMA FLYNT OF BEL AIR.
I'M SORRY, DID YOU RIDE A BIKE?
NO. I DON'T DO BUSINESS WITH STRANGE WOMEN ON BIKES.

WELL, I GUESS I HEARD WRONG THAT YOU WERE A MAN THAT LIKED TO DO BUSINESS.

BUSINESS, I LOVE. I DON'T JUST SELL MY... "ORCHIDS"...TO WEIRD WOMEN IN BIKE SHORTS THAT APPEAR ON MY DOORSTEP. NOW SHOO, CHILD, OR I SHALL ALERT THE CONSTABULARY.

OH THAT'S RICH--!

PLAN B.

THIS REALLY SHOULD HAVE BEEN "PLAN A" ALL ALONG.

IN FACT IN THE FUTURE WHATEVER MY FIRST PLAN IS--
--JUST GONNA AUTO-SCRAP IT.

FROM NOW ON PLAN B IS ALWAYS PLAN A.

PLAN A IS JUST, LIKE, THE GARBAGE PLAN. THE STUPID PLAN.

BECAUSE PLAN B ALWAYS JUST...

...ALWAYS...
WHOA.

MOMMA LIKE.

MOMMA LIKE A **LOT.**
SO SHE'S GONNA JUST **SAUNTER** ON OVER THERE AND--

!

WAIT, SO WHY DOES **BELLBOY-GIRL** THERE NOT HAVE TO WEAR A UNIFORM?
SHE AIN'T ONE OF **US,** DUMBY...

CARDS DOWN, BOYS.
TIME TO GO HELP OUR **GUEST** "CHECK OUT."

OH, THANK GOD.
I WAS STARTING TO FORGET HOW TO USE THIS.

GET HER!
OH MY GOD SHE SHOT ME WITH A FUTZING ARROW!

DON'T SHOOT THE FLOWER
DON'T SHOOT THE FLOWER
DON'T SHOOT THE FLOWER
DON'T SHOOT THE FLOWER
DON'T--

AWW, FLOWER--

FFUFHH

TCH TCH TCH.

TRESPASSING AND HARASSMENT.
GET HER GONE, MANOLO.
OLOYEDDS BODDS.

HEY!!
WEED BOSS

AAAARRRGH!

I JUST--I JUST--
I JUST WANT TO BREAK IN AND TAKE IT. LET HIM CALL THE COPS ON ME, I'LL BE THE PROBABLE CAUSE--
HEY, HEY, HOLD ON NOW...

...LOOK, KIDDO, AT MY BEST I'M BORDERLINE BUT IF WE'RE NO BETTER THAN THEM...

...THEN WE'RE NO BETTER THAN THEM.
Y'DIG?

DO BETTER. BE BETTER.

I AM BETTER THAN YOU, FLYNT WARD.

AND I'M GONNA PROVE IT.

I PEDAL AFTER "WEED LORD" ALL DAY.

GATHERING EVIDENCE.

KEEPING MY DISTANCE.

STRAIGHT.

UP.

CREEPIN'.

BUT IT IS DOWN THESE MEAN STREETS A NICE GIRL MUST GO IN PURSUIT OF THE EVIL WEED LORD.

THIS...
THIS LOOKS BAD.
THIS LOOKS SUPER
SUPER
BAAAAA--
OW
OW
OW OW OW
OW
SMILE, BUTTERCUP.
CLICK

BISHOP!

I SWEAR TO GOD YOU ARE LIKE A RASH OR A--
--LIKE A FUNGUS OR A MOLD THAT WON'T GO AWAY OR--
--LIKE A CHRONIC...PURPLE... MEDDLING...
PAIN IN MY ASS.
DETECTIVE CAUDLE, THAT MAN RAN ME OVER AND DROVE OFF. I HAVE PICTURES.
ALSO YOU SHOULD MAYBE HAVE YOUR ASS CHECKED OUT.

ALSO ALSO, I WOULD BE SHOCKED IF YOU TOLD ME HE HAD LIKE A TON OF WEED ON HIS PERSON.
I MEAN HIS TAG IS "WEED LORD" FOR CRYIN' OUT LOUD.

WHAT? HE'S LEGAL. IT'S LEGAL HERE. HE'S GOT HIS CARD AND PAPERS AND EVERYTHING.
THE HIT AND RUN IS A FELONY; THAT HE HAD A GUN GETS HIM A DIME JUST FOR SHOWING UP. PENAL CODE 12022.53. "USE A GUN AND YOU'RE DONE."

MR. WARD IS GOING AWAY BUT I HAVE A FEELING YOU WON'T BE.
AND THAT YOU THINK THIS IS THE START OF SOME KIND OF CHARMINGLY ANTAGONISTIC RELATIONSHIP AND THAT I'M GOING TO BE HELPING YOU OUT IN THE FUTURE.

WITH TIME YOU'LL FIND ME GRUFF BUT ENDEARING AS I'LL FIND YOU SPUNKY AND AGGRESSIVE BUT ULTIMATELY ON THE SIDE OF THE ANGELS.
AM I WRONG ABOUT... LITERALLY ANY OF THAT, MS. BISHOP?

HEY, I JUST HAVE ONE MORE THING TO TAKE CARE OF THEN I'M DONE. I'M GONE. I'M A GHOST.
I PROMISE.

MARCUS...?

YOU'RE NOT SUPPOSED TO SEE ME. IT'S BAD LUCK.
BAD LUCK LIKE OUR FLORIST LOSES ALL OUR FLOWERS TWO DAYS BEFORE THE WEDDING?
OR WORSE?

BABY, I KNOW YOU HAD THIS THING IN YOUR HEAD YOU WANTED TODAY TO BE. I KNOW YOU DID. AND I DID TOO--
--OR AT LEAST I KNEW I WANTED WHATEVER YOU WANTED. BUT MARCUS...

IT'S TODAY THAT MATTERS. IT'S YOU THAT MATTERS--YOU AND ME--AND NOT THE FLOWERS OR OUR FAMILIES OR FRIENDS...
I'LL TAKE YOU TO VEGAS AND MARRY YOU THERE, OR PARIS OR MONTE CARLO--
I'LL TAKE YOU AROUND THE WORLD AND MARRY YOU EVERY TIME THE PLANE TOUCHES THE GROUND AS LONG AS IT MEANS LAST NIGHT WAS THE LAST NIGHT I HAVE TO ENDURE NOT BEING YOUR HUSBAND ANYMORE.

IT WAS SUCH A STORYBOOK IN MY HEAD. AFTER ALL THIS TIME I JUST WANTED YOU TO HAVE A STORYBOOK AND--
OH, HONEY.
YOU ARE MY HAPPILY EVER AFTER.

HEY, NEIGHBORS.

I GOT ONE.

THERE'S MY GIRL!
HEYYY... YOU.

OW
I'M PROUD OF YA, KID.
THANKSOW--
THE BAD GUY GOT GOT--THAT'S WHAT MATTERS.
THE GOOD GUYS WON AND WE WON BY THE RULES.

I TOOK A LIBERTY OR TWO--YOU'LL NEED THESE.
SOME FILES. THOSE ARE, UH. THOSE ARE FOR YOUR FILES. WRITE EVERYTHING DOWN. EVERYTHING. PUT IT ALL IN THESE.
AND THESE INDEX CARDS. THE REAL TRICKY CASES--YOU PUT WHAT YOU KNOW DOWN ON THESE AND MOVE 'EM AROUND. SEE WHAT HAPPENS.

AWW, THANK YOU, CAT FOOD MAN.
THIS IS ACTUALLY REALLY SWEET.

HEY, I ACTUALLY DON'T EVEN KNOW YOUR--

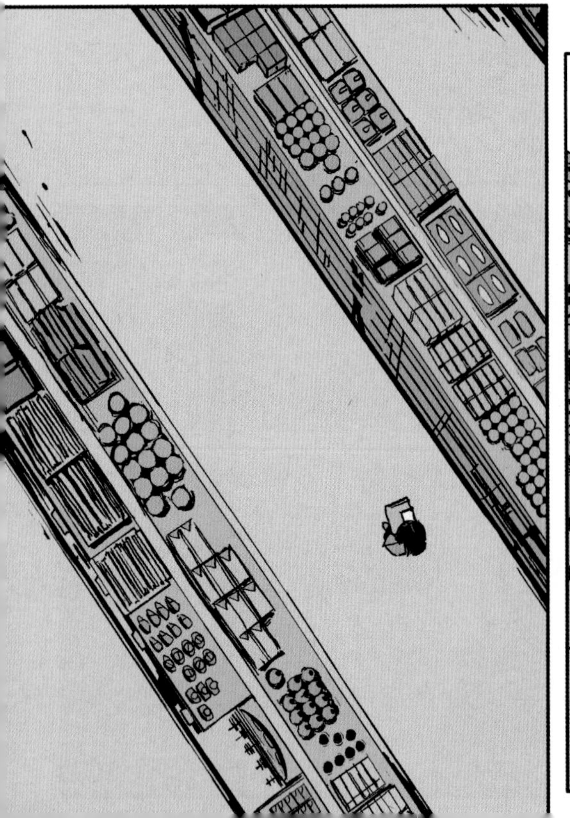

EXCUSE ME, DID YOU SEE THAT GUY TAKE OFF? TRENCHCOAT, FACE KIND OF LIKE A BASSET HOUND, SHUFFLES AND MUMBLES A LOT?
PURPLE LADY, YOU BEEN THE ONLY PERSON HERE FOR THE LAST HALF-HOUR EASY.
99¢

99¢
MAYBE I GOT A CONCUSSION.

WARD.
FLYNT WARD.
YEAH.
PHONE CALL TIME. C'MON.
IF YOU NEED LEGAL REPRESENTATION I HAVE A LIST OF--
--I DO NOT, THANK YOU VERY MUCH.
IT'S WARD. PUT ME THROUGH.
I FOUND HER.
SHE GOT ME ARRESTED BUT I FOUND HER.
I TRIED RUNNING HER OVER AND SHE TOOK A DAMN SELFIE, THAT'S HOW.
I'M FRUSTRATED. IT'S BEEN A LONG NIGHT. BUT I WANTED YOU TO BE MY FIRST CALL...

"...MADAME MASQUE."
YES, WELL. YOU ALWAYS WERE A BRIGHT BOY.
AND YES. THE ORCHIDS WERE LOVELY.
THEY'RE A LOVELY DETAIL TO MY EVENING BATH. I SHALL REQUIRE MORE.
AND TELL ME WHAT YOU KNOW ABOUT MS. BISHOP...

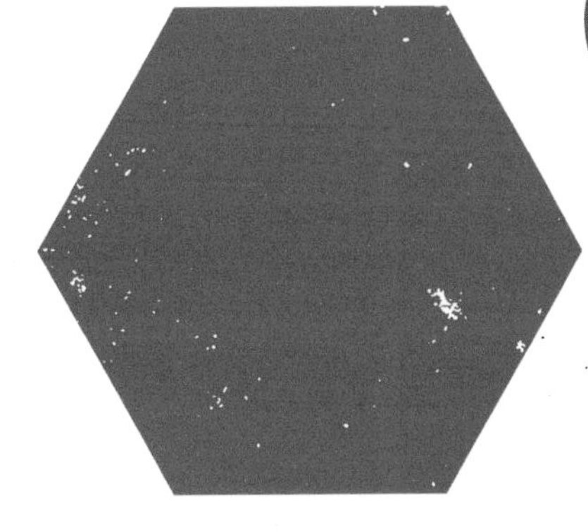

fun & games

R L E E A X U M H E C K E

G U F R A C T I O N C H G

L L W D O A J A C A H N D

H Y B R O L L T R E P M A

S O F D E H A W K E Y E M

L N L Q J R Z A I D B O A

I I K L B D S C A D R L N

E Z E R I A A K V M E O A

G L P B C N F E A C N P T

R Z I R E I G R R H N P C

U D F O E R Q S S T A P A

E E G W P A R D W U N M L

N R E N C O H C U O U M M

W M B O S S U N G P R E S

A O O O D P U L I D O T Q

L F F R F R A R O I N G H

D V K K B C Z I I S O I N

Okay...

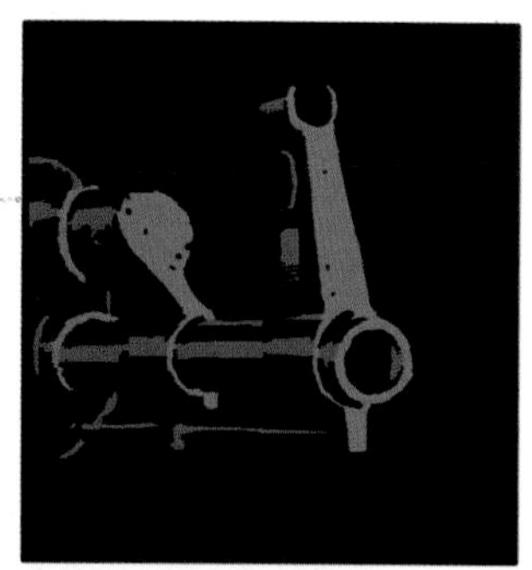

This looks...

completely ridiculous.
Whatever happens to me tonight? However bad it gets?
I had it comin'.

BRO.
GET IN VAN, BRO.
JUST GO, BRO.

Sure thing, fellas.

sure

thing.
CAN I PULL UP MY DRAWS FIRST?

ABSOLUTELY MOTHERFUTZING NOT BRO.
BROOOOOOOO. VAN NOW, BRO, OKAY, BRO.

Come on, Barton.
Come on--

GUYS, WANNA SEE A MAGIC TRICK?

FIVE-SIX-SEVEN *LETTERS,* STARTS WITH B, ENDS WITH E.

"ALL THE STUFF YOU TAKE WITH YOU."

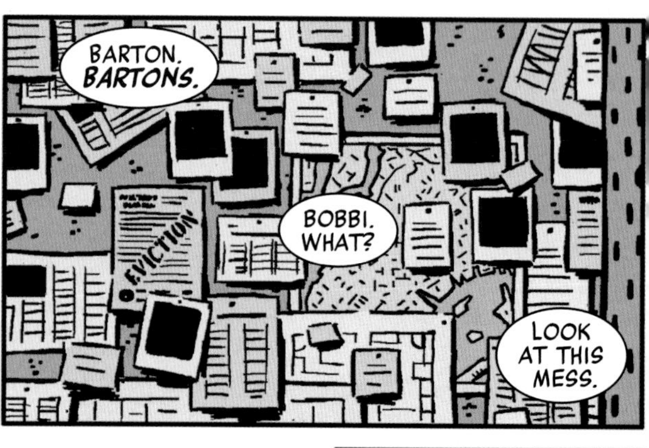

FUN and GAMES

BY **MATT FRACTION** AND **DAVID AJA** WITH **MATT HOLLINGSWORTH** AND **CHRIS ELIOPOULOS**

--WHAT'S THE MATTER WITH *YOU?*

I BROKE MY BELT.

PEOPLE THAT GET LEFT WITH A SOGGY WET STICK.

SO DO YOU KNOW ANYTHING ABOUT THESE GUYS?
RUSSIAN? SLAVIC? MAYBE SOME POLISH?
ACCENTS AND DIALECTS ALL OVER THE MAP.
I PULLED THE RECORDS OF THAT STRIP CLUB YOU BUSTED UP.
CLINT...
HOW DID YOU KNOW ABOUT THAT?
OKAY, OKAY, I'M SORRY. WHAT.
I WASN'T THERE FOR THE GIRLS I WAS THERE FOR THE GUYS.
NO WAIT.
EIGHT LETTERS. "A MALE RAPPER."
In Brooklyn
Real Estate
Unknown Arm of
Is Uncovered in
WELL, IT'S OWNED BY A SHELL COMPANY.
LIKE--
LIKE A FAKE COMPANY. A TAX DODGE.
THAT WAS WRAPPED IN ANOTHER AND ANOTHER BUT EVENTUALLY I GOT A NAME.
"IVAN BANIONIS."
"OKAY LET'S GO GET HIM."
"CAN'T, YOU GOT HIM DEPORTED."
United States
EVICTION NOTICE
"HE, OR HIS COMPANIES, OR HIS COMPANY'S COMPANIES, OWN BUILDINGS.
"ALL OVER THE PLACE. ALL OVER THE CITY.
"ALL OVER THIS BLOCK, CLINT.
UH-OH.
"CLINT, THEY OWN EVERY BUILDING FOR THREE BLOCKS IN EVERY DIRECTION BUT YOURS.
"DO YOU REALIZE THE TIME AND MONEY AND WILLPOWER THAT TOOK THESE GUYS, CLINT?"
home sales
YOU HAVE ANY IDEA HOW BIG A PAIN IN THE ASS YOU ARE TO THEM?
"ENVELOPES"?
I DON'T GET IT.

SURROUNDED, BRO.
VAN, BRO.
BRO, HE SHOOT YOU, BRO, SO YOU GO, BRO YOU GO--
C'MON, C'MON--
ONE TRICK, ONE TIME.

YOU GUYS MIGHT BE MY LAST AUDIENCE EVER, RIGHT? COME ON.
JUST SAY THE MAGIC WORD.

...IS...
...IS "ABRA CADABRA"?

"BARNEY."

WHAT YOU SAY, BRO?
"BARNEY," SAY "BARNEY."

"BARNEY."

NO, NO, COME ON, IT'S A MAGIC TRICK AND I GOT MY PANTS DOWN.
YOU GOTTA SHOUT IT.

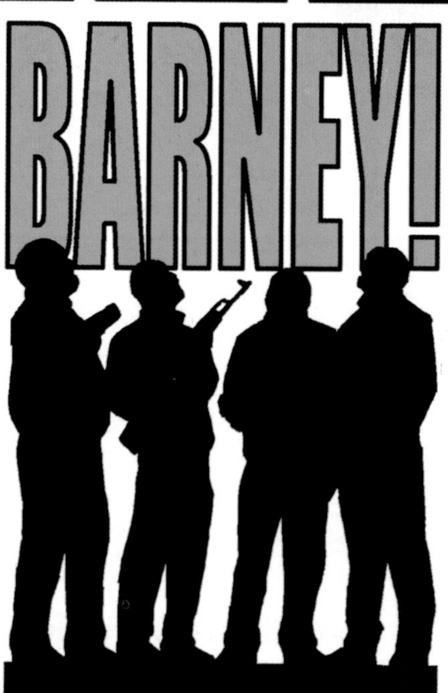
BARNEY!

THANKS, BRO.

TONG

GRRRAAAAAHHHH!!

BARTON...

WHAT IS THIS?

NAT, THIS'S--

I KNOW QUITE WELL YOUR BROTHER BARTON, BARTON.
WHY IS HE WITH US?
JUST SPARING THE PRICE OF A CUPPA COFFEE FOR A FELLOW AMERICAN DOWN ON HIS LUCK.
MORE COFFE

≈SIGH≈
YOUR DOSSIER.

MM.

WHAT ARE YOU TWO IDIOTS DOING?

MM.

YOU'RE THE ONE DOING ALL THIS CLOAK-AND-DAGGER STUFF WITH THE HAT AND THE JACKET AND YOUR FANCY-ASS DOSSIER.
ARE WE BEING TAILED?
ARE WE BEING WATCHED?
WHAT "CLOAK-AND-DAGGER" STUFF? THIS IS JUST HAT.

She's lying, of course, but she knows I know she's lying so that's okay.
She dug up **eighteen killings** in the tri-state alone so maybe a little cloak-and-dagger isn't the worst idea.
FIVE LETTERS, COMIC ENTERTAINER.
HMM. L-E-W-I-S?
NO...AHH, OKAY.
GIC
HOBO
R
CLOW
THE WEAPONS CHANGE SOMETIMES, SCENE TO SCENE, BUT SHOT PATTERN IS CONSISTENT.
AND THERE IS A SYMBOL ALWAYS, SOMEWHERE NEARBY.
VICTIMS ALL HAVE TIES TO *TITUSHKI*--TO TRACKSUITS--
--AND THE VICTIMS ALL STOOD IN THEIR WAY.
MAN.
"NO. ***HIT***MAN.
"AND HE HAS PERFECT NEGATIVE SPACE AROUND HIM--SO HE IS UNAFRAID.
"BECAUSE HE KNOWS HIS NAME MEANS NOTHING.
"HE IS NOT EVEN A SHADOW. NOT EVEN A GHOST--
"HE'S BLANK.
"HE'S JUST A ***SHAPE.***"
I THINK YOU'RE BEING HUNTED BY A KILLER THAT CAN SIGN HIS WORK AS LARGELY AND AS LOUDLY AS HE LIKES...

"...BECAUSE NOBODY KNOWS ANYTHING ABOUT HIM."
KAZU...
YES, SIR?
IT'S MAGNIFICENT. YOU AND YOUR TEAM HAVE DONE IT AGAIN.
THANK YOU, SIR.
ENTIRE CONTENT OF THE NEIGHBORHOOD CHANGES WHILE THE FUNDAMENTAL FORM OF ITS FOOTPRINT REMAINS.
MM. MM-HM. MM-HM.
CEST M. BISHOP AVEC LE GROUPE
LADIES AND GENTLEMEN, LET'S BEGIN.
SIR.
HIHOWAREYA.
IT'S A THREE BLOCK BY THREE BLOCK PARCEL OF LAND.
AND IT'S ABOUT TO BECOME MANHATTAN'S PREMIER LUXURY SHOPPING DESTINATION.
THE NEIGHBORHOOD AS IT STANDS IS LOWER AND MIDDLE INCOME HOUSING, A FEW BODEGAS, AND A LOT OF DEAD REAL ESTATE.
AND IF THERE'S ONE THING MANHATTAN HATES, IT'S THAT.
WE HAVE, WITH YOUR INVESTMENT DOLLARS, ACQUIRED ALL THE VARIOUS BUILDINGS AND PARCELS OF LAND.
WELL.
BUT ONE.

THAT SAID, WE'RE IN THE PROCESS OF--
--IT WON'T--
--THE BUILDING WILL BE ACQUIRED. WE'VE EXPERIENCED A BRIEF DELAY IN BEGINNING CONSTRUCTION AND DEMOLITION BUT--
DAMMIT, STEVE--
YOU ASSURED US YOU HAD THIS HANDLED. WE HAVE DEADLINES FOR THE CONSTRUCTION TEAMS THAT HAVE TO BE MET--
--CONTRACTORS RETAINED, THE DAMN UNIONS AND--

EXCUSE ME, GENTLEMEN.

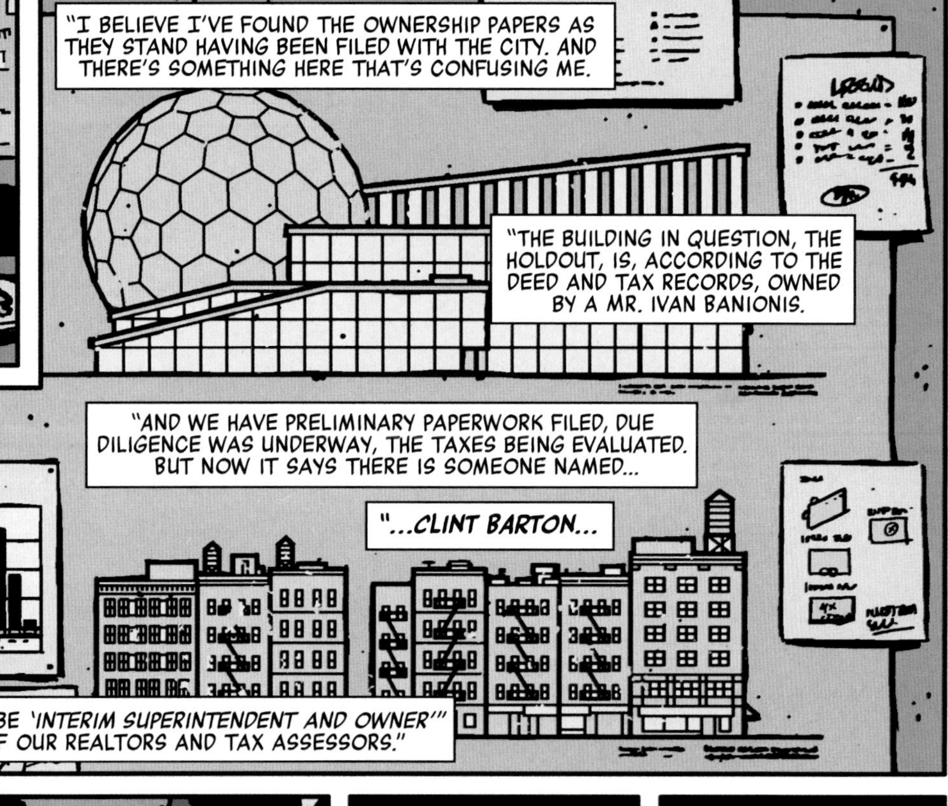

"I BELIEVE I'VE FOUND THE OWNERSHIP PAPERS AS THEY STAND HAVING BEEN FILED WITH THE CITY. AND THERE'S SOMETHING HERE THAT'S CONFUSING ME.
"THE BUILDING IN QUESTION, THE HOLDOUT, IS, ACCORDING TO THE DEED AND TAX RECORDS, OWNED BY A MR. IVAN BANIONIS.
"AND WE HAVE PRELIMINARY PAPERWORK FILED, DUE DILIGENCE WAS UNDERWAY, THE TAXES BEING EVALUATED. BUT NOW IT SAYS THERE IS SOMEONE NAMED...
"...CLINT BARTON...
"...CLAIMING TO BE 'INTERIM SUPERINTENDENT AND OWNER'" CHASING OFF OUR REALTORS AND TAX ASSESSORS."

WHAT THE HELL DOES THAT HAVE TO DO WITH--

"INTERIM SUPERINTENDENT AND OWNER"?
THAT DOESN'T SOUND TERRIBLY LEGAL TO ME.

LADIES AND GENTLEMEN...
...THE PROBLEM WILL BE RESOLVED IMMINENTLY. YOU SEE...

"BARTON IS BREAKING THE LAW."
RABBIT COMES OUT OF THE HOLE,
...GOES AROUND...

OOP

AWW, PANTS--

CLCK
BRO.

WE GOT YOU NOW AGAIN, BRO.
INTO VAN YOU GO, BRO.
GIVE BOW, BRO, AND ARROW, BRO.
GUYS GUYS GUYS GUYS GUYS GUYS GUYS--

CAN'T A GUY TIE HIS PANTS UP ONE TIME BEFORE WE GET INTO IT?

VAN, BRO.
NOW, BRO. AND YOU SHUT UP TOO, BRO.

Thor doesn't have to deal with crap like this I bet.
ALL RIGHT, ALL RIGHT.
I wish I was Thor. I wish I could smash this guy in the face with a hammer.

Wish I could hit myself in the face with a hammer.
Wish I was anyone else.
Anywhere else.

WHAT YOU MEAN, BRO? DAS CRAZY.
XXX
БОЛВАНЫ TOWN

SHUT UP, MORON.

LET THE BRO FINISH.

AS I WAS SAYING...

IT IS AN ILLEGAL-- AN UNLAWFUL-- OCCUPATION.
BARTON HAS NO MORE RIGHTS TO BE PRESENT ON YOUR PROPERTY THAN A SQUATTER OR DEADBEAT TENANT.
BUT WHAT THAT MEAN, BRO?

TT.

"IT MEANS MY EARLIER CAUTION IN PLAYING THIS LITTLE...
"GAME OF OURS...
SUBJECT: Clint Barton
ALIAS: "Hawkeye"
LAST NAME Barton
WEIGHT
NAME Clinton
DATE OF B
JUNE 18,
BIRTHPLAC
Do NOT
Spider-Woman ??
Mockingbird

"...WAS LARGELY UNFOUNDED.
New York City Po
NAME: BARTON, CL
"THE GOOD GUY IT SEEMS IS NOT SO GOOD."

HEH.
HE SAYING, THE BRO CANNOT CALL THE COPS.

PRECISELY.
AND NOW TO WIN THE GAME.

S'NOT TOO SMART, MAN.
Shut up, Barney.

I MEAN, THEY JUST WAIT OUT HERE FOR YOU?
SOMETHING'S NOT RIGHT.
Shut--

--oh.
CLINNNNNNNNNNT!

OF COURSE he's right.

BARNEY.
ELEVATOR.

HUP.

c'mon
c'mon
C'MON

remember
kids
space
blind corn--

--dammit--

BLAM
DAMMIT

BLAMM

BLAM

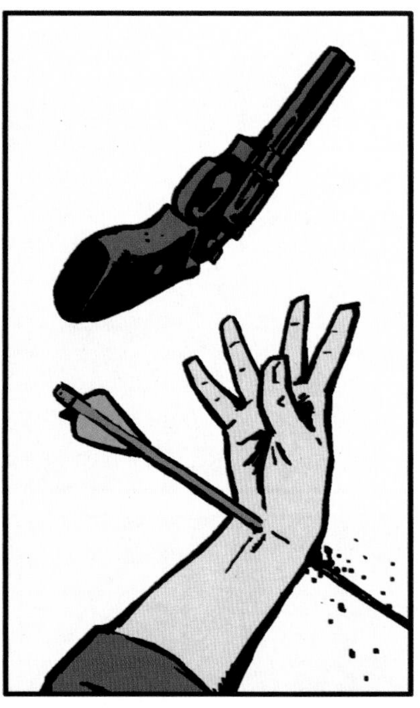

SIMONE!

DON'T DO IT, BRO. I GOT KID, BRO.

JUST SAY THE MAGIC WORD.

UH.
NO?

KASHHH

MOMMA!!

BABIES.
COME HERE, BABIES. MOMMA GOT YOU.

YOU GUYS OKAY?

SORRY ABOUT THAT. OUR GUESTS DIDN'T, UH...
GUESS YOU COULD SAY THOSE GUYS REALLY...THEY REALLY...

THOSE TWO GUYS, THEY...
THEY, UH...

I THREW 'EM OFF THE FIRE ESCAPE.

YOU CAN'T--
BUT I DID, JESS.

--CLINT--
--DAMMIT--
--YOU CAN'T **NOT CALL THE COPS** BECAUSE YOU THINK YOU CAN JUST CALL **THE AVENGERS** AND **SKATE** ON **GOOD INTENTIONS.**

YOU DO THE RIGHT THING RIGHT? OKAY?
YOU SEE A THING, IT'S WRONG, YOU THINK--
--YOU THINK **NO,** I'M GOING TO MAKE THAT **RIGHT.**
SO YOU **DO IT** AND... AND...
...THE RULES GET IN THE WAY SO YOU DON'T?

NO. I'M GOING TO DO THE RIGHT THING AND I DON'T--
--THEY WERE GOING TO KICK THESE FOLKS **OUT,** JESS, AND JUST--
--I JUST WANTED TO DO SOMETHING RIGHT.

IT'S NOT THAT SIMPLE, CLINT.
YEAH, BUT IT SHOULD BE.

HEY, CLINT?
WHAT, BARNEY?

SO HOW'D THEY GET IN?

WE HAD THE PLACE ON LOCKDOWN, YEAH?
WITH ALLA YOUR LITTLE DEPUTIES RUNNING AROUND.

"YOU HAD THOSE TWO GUYS OUT BACK."

...AND WE WERE OUT FRONT, STOPPING THE OTHER JERKS.
HM.

"AND BEFORE THAT, YOU HAD THE DOOR COVERED.

"AND I WATCHED IT WHEN YOU WERE GONE."

So they would have had to have had...
THE ROOF.
THEY WERE ALREADY INSIDE.

"THEY MIGHT STILL BE INSIDE--"
EXIT

DAMMIT--
--DAMMIT--
--CLINT, YOU MORON--

too late

we're too

always too late

WARNING
High voltage

16

THIS TAPE IS RECORDED:
AT ☐ 1⅞ ☐ 3¾ ☐ 7½ ☐ 15
☐ MONOPHONIC
☒ STEREOPHONIC

SUNSET BLVD. HOLLYWOOD 28 CALIF.

PROGRAM: HAWKEYE
CLIENT: MATT FRACTION REV
ARTIST: ANNIE WU
ENGINEER: MATT HOLLINGSWORTH
2nd ENGR.: CHRIS ELIOPOULOS — TAPE MCH. NO.: — TAPE SPEED: — C. O. NO.:
EDITED BY: DAVID AJA — DATE: — REMARKS:

SPOT OR MASTER NO.	R. R. MASTER NO.	TITLE	TIME
SW/TB 416		-SIDE 1-	
		. LUCKY	3:24
		. VAGABOND CODE	3:05
		. CHERRY	3:46
		. THE TAPE	2:33
		. THE TAPE (TAKE 2)	2:59
		. SIX DAYS IN THE LIFE OF	3:07
		. SANDY	2:46
		. MY BAD PENNY	3:12
		. GIRLS	3:08
		Total by Clock........	

A-FINE

(ORIGINAL MASTER)

REMARKS:
MASTERS BY: — DATE: — STUDIO: — SEC. — ROW — BIN

F-272 5-54

Time Chart

TAPE LENGTH	SINGLE TRACK 3¾ ips	SINGLE TRACK 7½ ips	DUAL TRACK 3¾ ips	DUAL TRACK 7½ ips
1200 FT.	1 hr.	30 min.	2 hr.	1 hr.
1800 FT.	1 hr. 30 min.	45 min.	3 hr.	1 hr. 30 min.
2400 FT.	2 hr.	1 hr.	4 hr.	2 hr.

A J A

Once upon a time...

Once upon a time in ***Los Angeles...***

Once upon a time in Los Angeles a sad boy sang a song.

And when he finished, he hit an E chord as hard as his big little fingers would let him.

46 YEARS LATER AND NO ONE HAS HEARD HIM PLAY ANOTHER NOTE.
BEEEP
HONK HONK
HONK
HONK
HONK
BEEP
BEEP BEEP
BEEEP
AND SO IT CAME TO PASS THAT THE ENTIRETY OF EVERYONE ON THE 405 WAS NOT PISSED AT ME FOR LITERALLY THE FIRST TIME SINCE I CAME OUT HERE.
APPARENTLY LOS ANGELES ISN'T SO INTO SHARING THE ROAD.
OR ANYTHING NOT A CAR.
ANYWHERE.
AWW, MAN...
HEY, BUDDY!
HEY!
HONK
BEEP
HONK
BEEP
BEEEP

GONE, GONE.
'S ALL GONE.
UM. WHAT?
WOMAN!
WOMAN!

IT'S STOLEN, IT ALL GOT STOLEN, THEY'RE GONE.
EASY NOW, GUY, WHAT'S GONE?
WOMAN! YOU!
HEY!
YOU CAN'T LEAN YOUR BIKE ON MY--

IT'S HIM, HE'S STILL TRYING TO GET ME
HE KEEPS REPEATING THE SAME, LIKE, NINE WORDS IN DIFFERENT ORDER BASICALLY.
SOMEBODY STOLE SOMETHING FROM HIM AND IT'S GONE FOREVER.

PLEASE, SIR, CAN YOU AT LEAST DO THIS NOT ON FOOT IN THE PASSING LANE?
LET ME GET YOU A BOTTLE OF WATER OR--

NO!!

NO.

I'M SORRY I DIDN'T RESPECT YOUR PERSONAL SPACE, SIR.
START SLOWLY. HELP ME UNDERSTAND.
WHO STOLE WHAT FROM YOU, SIR?

AND IF I GOT IT BACK FOR YOU, WOULD YOU PAY ME?
WILL BRYSON?!?

WHO?
ME.
HIM.
WHO?
WILL BRYSON.
HELLO.
WRRF.

HEY.
BABY GIRL, YOU ARE A BABY, GIRL. DO YOU REALLY NOT KNOW WHO WILL BRYSON IS?
HE'S...THIS GUY?
HE WAS THE SIXTIES, GIRL!

HE AND HIS BROTHER GREY WERE THE BRYSON BROTHERS. AND THEY WERE THE CALIFORNIA SOUND BEFORE THERE WAS A CALIFORNIA SOUND.
THEY MIXED HARMONIES AND DOO-WOP AND WHITE SOUL SENSIBILITIES WITH PRODUCTION WORK THAT MADE THEIR LITTLE TEENAGE LOVE SONGS SOUND HUGE...
BUT LIKE LOVE THEY NEVER MADE IT OUT OF L.A. IN ONE PIECE, LET ALONE THE SIXTIES.
DRUG AND MENTAL ILLNESS AND BIG WEIRDNESS SNUFFED THEIR CAREERS BEFORE THEY STARTED.
THEY COULD'VE BEEN THE AMERICAN BEATLES, KATE.

AND THAT'S YOU? THE AMERICAN BEATLE?

YEAH YEAH YEAH.

WELL I CALLED THE NUMBER ON HIS MEDICAL BRACELET AND HIS "NURSING STAFF" IS ON THE WAY.
MR. BRYSON, WE'RE BOTH HUGE FANS.

WAIT, YOU CAN'T JUST--
--WHAT GOT STOLEN?
MY WISH.
THE THING THAT BROKE ME.

"'WISH' IS HIS LOST MASTERWORK, KATE. IT WAS THE RECORD HE COULD NEVER FINISH. THEY WENT INTO THEIR RECORDING STUDIO AND NEVER CAME OUT.
"MUSICIANS WOULD SWEAR THEY PLAYED SESSIONS IN ANONYMOUS STUDIOS. SNIPPETS OF TAPE WOULD SNEAK OUT. WHISPERS OF LIVE SECRET SHOWS CONDUCTED BEHIND MASKS...
"AND THERE WAS SOME SISYPHIAN PROJECT THEY WERE RUMORED TO BE MAKING.
"AND MAKING."
AND MAKING.

"YEAH, THAT'S MY 'WISH.' I GOT--
"WELL, I'VE BEEN RECORDING STUFF BUT NONE OF IT'S READY, IT'S ALL SKETCHES AND NOW...
"MODERN PRODUCTION, RIGHT? IT'S ALL BEEN DIGITIZED AND SOMEONE STOLE AND LEAKED SOME OF THE DIGITAL FILES.
"NOW THEY'RE ALL GOING TO COME OUT AND ITS MY OWN BROTHER'S FAULT."
KNOCK. KNOCK.
HE'S JUST TRYING TO MAKE ME LOOK BAD AND SAD AND EMBARRASSED--

UM.
'SUP?

I BEG YOUR PARDON WE'RE HERE TO COLLECT MR. BRYSON.
A MISTER FINCH REPORTED HIM HERE.

I WAS ALWAYS BETTER THAN HIM AND NOW GREY'S GONNA PUNISH ME. HE KNOWS I'M A FAILURE AND NOW HE WANTS EVERYONE ELSE TO KNOW--
--HE'S GOING TO TELL EVERYONE I'M UNWELL.

HEY--
HEY!
MA'AM, PLEASE. WE HAVE THIS SITUATION COVERED.

THE HELL YOU DO, THX-1138!
GUY DOESN'T WANT TO GO, HE DOESN'T HAVE TO--
WILL? WILL!
MR. BRYSON, YOU DON'T--

HE'LL HAVE BEEN SEDATED BY NOW, MA'AM. NO REASON TO YELL.
Y'ALL LOOK A LOT LIKE A BUNCHA BLEACHED-OUT BELLBOYS, Y'KNOW THAT?

TCH.

KATIE, PLEASE, HONEY, STAND DOWN. THEY LOOKED LIKE THEY WERE ABOUT TO HIT YOU.

I SMELL A CASE.

OKAY, SELF-FLAGEL-KATE-TION--TIME TO GET YOUR LIBARRY ON.

AK-A-TAK-A-TAK-A-TAK-A-TAK-A-TAK-A-TAK-A-TAK-A-TAK-A-TA

COMPUTERS RUIN EVERYTHING.
COMPUTERS ARE THE WORST.

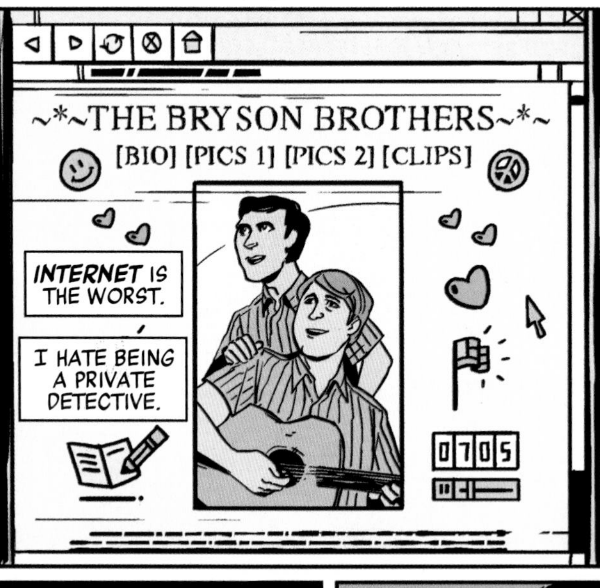
~*~THE BRYSON BROTHERS~*~
[BIO] [PICS 1] [PICS 2] [CLIPS]
INTERNET IS THE WORST.
I HATE BEING A PRIVATE DETECTIVE.
0705

HM.

EXCUSE ME.

I WAS WONDERING IF YOU GUYS COULD TURN OFF YOUR FIREWALL FOR A SECOND?
I'M TRYING TO RUN A P2P CLIENT TO FILESHARE SOME EVIDENCE BUT BETWEEN THAT AND YOUR JANKY NAT SETTINGS, IT'S NOT WORKING.

CAN YOU HELP ME STEAL SOME MUSIC OFF THE INTERNET?

OH COME ON--

OH, COME ON--

--YOU AGAIN?!
WHAT "ME AGAIN?" WHY? I'M GREAT.
JUST THE NURSE RATCHET OF DOWNEY DIDN'T THINK SO.

KID, WHAT ARE YOU DOING, CAUSING A RUCKUS AT THE DAMN LIBRARY...?
I ASKED A VERY SIMPLE QUESTION OF A WOMAN WHO IN THEORY IS SUPPOSED TO FACILITATE AVAILABILITY OF INFORMATION AND SUDDENLY EVERYBODY'S METALLICA'S DRUMMER.
AND WHAT, PRAY TELL, INFORMATION IS THE SYSTEM STANDING IN THE WAY OF?

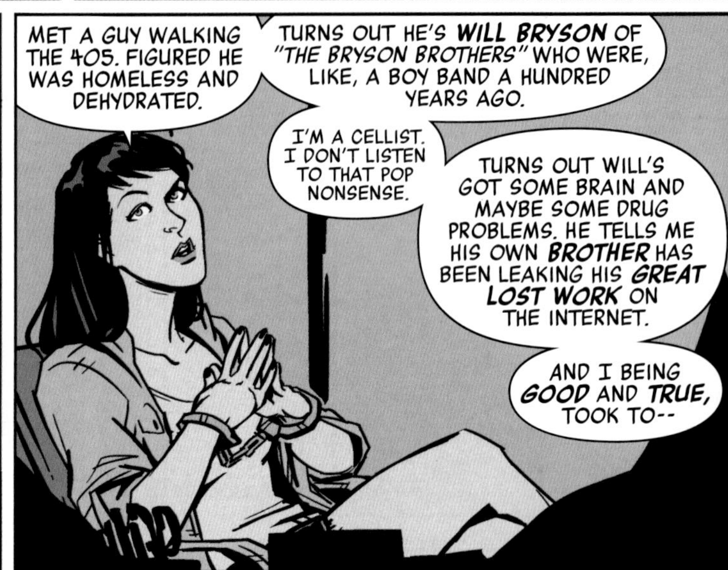
MET A GUY WALKING THE 405. FIGURED HE WAS HOMELESS AND DEHYDRATED.
TURNS OUT HE'S WILL BRYSON OF "THE BRYSON BROTHERS" WHO WERE, LIKE, A BOY BAND A HUNDRED YEARS AGO.
I'M A CELLIST. I DON'T LISTEN TO THAT POP NONSENSE.
TURNS OUT WILL'S GOT SOME BRAIN AND MAYBE SOME DRUG PROBLEMS. HE TELLS ME HIS OWN BROTHER HAS BEEN LEAKING HIS GREAT LOST WORK ON THE INTERNET.
AND I BEING GOOD AND TRUE, TOOK TO--

ALL RIGHT, I'VE HEARD ENOUGH.
WILL AND GREY BRYSON. OY.

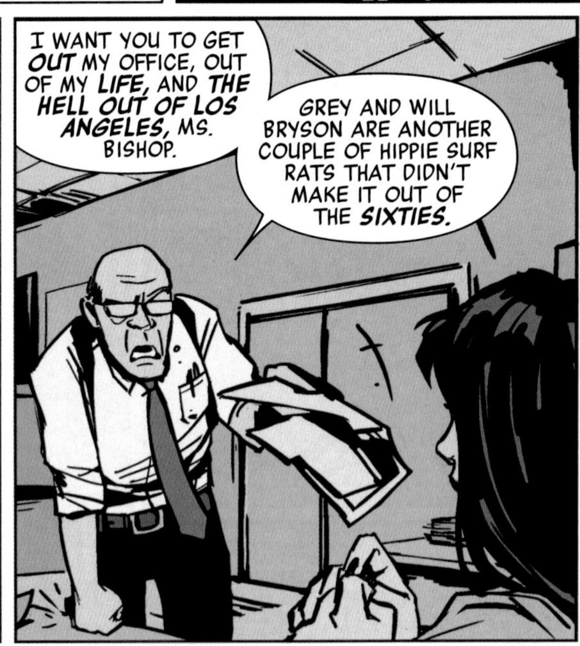
I WANT YOU TO GET OUT MY OFFICE, OUT OF MY LIFE, AND THE HELL OUT OF LOS ANGELES, MS. BISHOP.
GREY AND WILL BRYSON ARE ANOTHER COUPLE OF HIPPIE SURF RATS THAT DIDN'T MAKE IT OUT OF THE SIXTIES.

DON'T LET THEM TAKE YOU DOWN WITH THEM.

THEY'RE TABLOID FREAKS AND YOU SHOULD LEAVE THEM BOTH ALONE.

"TABLOID." BINGO.

...AND COMING UP ON OUR LEFT IS THE ONE-TIME HIPPIE HIDEAWAY HOME TO MILLIONAIRE ROCK AND ROLL RECLUSES **WILL** AND **GREY BRYSON...**

...OR, AS IT WAS KNOWN IN 1967, "THE HOUSE THAT LSD AND A HALF-MILLION DOLLARS BUILT"...

TMI CELEBRITY HOME TOURS

EVER SINCE THE SUMMER OF LOVE MUSIC INDUSTRY WAGS AND CELEBRITY WATCHERS HAVE WONDERED, WHICH OF THE ONE-TIME SQUEAKY CLEAN BRYSON BOYS WOULD KILL THE OTHER FIRST?

I HAVE **MY** MONEY ON CHRISTMAS EVE MURDER-SUICIDE.

OH LOOK EVERYBODY! IT'S CHER....

...'S UNCLE'S HOUSE.

CULTURE WILL BE THE DEATH OF US ALL.

IT'S LIKE IF MIKE BRADY DESIGNED THE BATES MOTEL.
IF I HAD TO LIVE HERE FOR 60 YEARS I BET I'D HAVE GONE FULL SYD BARRETT BY NOW M'SELF...

BUT THE GOOD NEWS IS THAT THE HOUSE IS STILL EXISTING VERY MUCH IN A PRE-TATE/LABIANCA SECURITY WORLD--

--SO GETTING INSIDE IS CAKE.

LOOK AT THESE GUYS--
--LOOKING AT HOW THEY GREW UP, GREW OLD, AND GREW WEIRD--

--IT'S LIKE YOU CAN WATCH THE FIFTIES TURN INTO THE SIXTIES.

WOULDN'T IT BE NI--

--WHOA.
A.S.C.A.P.?
YOU'LL WISH.
CAN WE HELP YOU?

HOLY CRAP, IT'S HERCULES, ICEMAN, BLACK WIDOW, GHOST RIDER, AND ANGEL!
BUT **WHY?** IT MAKES NO **SENSE!**
TOUR
1971

IT'S **WHAT--**
LIVE

OH **COME ON,** STEVE.

CRAP CRAP CRAP **CRAP--**

OH, HEY.

UM.
WILL?

OH, HEY.

SO THIS IS MY STUDIO, MAN... MY, UH...
NOBODY EVER BOTHERS ME IN HERE. THEY'LL NEVER EVEN KNOCK.
I DUNNO, MAYBE IT'S TOO WEIRD FOR 'EM.
IS, UM.
IS THAT A BJÖSENDURBER PIANO SITTING IN A GIANT WADING POOL?
NO, IT'S THE BJÖSENDURBER PIANO SITTING IN A GIANT WADING POOL. IT WAS THEIR FIRST ONE.
I DON'T KNOW WHO MADE THE WADING POOL.
DID YOU COME HERE TO HELP ME GET MY MUSIC BACK?
BECAUSE IF SO, I GOTTA SHOW YOU THE SCENE OF THE CRIME.
AND THIS IS... WHAT?
THIS IS IT. THIS IS MY "WISH." ACETATE MASTERS OF EVERY SECOND OF EVERY TAKE OF EVERY SESSION I'VE RECORDED SINCE I STARTED IN 1966.
A BIG CHUNK OF THE SEVENTIES AND 1995 WERE STOLEN AND PUT ON THE INTERNET.
NONE OF THE LABELS HAVE ANY WRITING ON THEM. HOW CAN YOU TELL WHAT'S WHAT?
I CAN TELL.
THIS IS THE HORN SECTION FANFARE FROM THE SECOND BRIDGE IN "BABY I GOT NO TIME TO RUN," RECORDED MAY 8TH, 1980.

OUR DAD, HE HIT US A LOT, SEE.
HE WAS A SESSION GUY. YOU KNOW "CARNIVAL RIDE"? THAT BIG HORN BIT IN THE MIDDLE, BWOMMP!
THAT WAS HIM. ANYWAY...
HE PUSHED ME AND GREY INTO MUSIC. GREY TOOK TO THE MIXING AND PRODUCTION AND ENGINEERING. IT WAS A WORLD HE COULD FINALLY CONTROL, RIGHT?
BUT ME...
...I IMAGINED A BETTER WORLD, ONE NOTE AT A TIME. IT WAS ALL I COULD DO.
AND "WISH" WAS SUPPOSED TO BE EVERYTHING, RIGHT? MY EVERYTHING. MY GRAND STATEMENT.
THE SIXTIES, RIGHT, OKAY, THE SIXTIES--
THEY CAME AFTER THE FIFTIES, RIGHT? AFTER THE FORTIES AFTER THE DAMN EIGHTEEN-EIGHTIES.
WE TURNED ON. OUR EYES OPENED. AND WE HAD SO MUCH TO ATONE FOR.
WE FINALLY FELT LOVE AND WERE LOVE AND WERE LOVED AND IN THE MIDDLE OF ALL THAT BEAUTY... I REALIZED WE HAD ALL DONE SO MUCH WRONG.
I WANTED TO MAKE A RECORD THAT HELD BOTH OF THOSE IDEAS. LOVE AT THIS TERRIBLE COST.
AND I WISHED WE'D NEVER FORGOT THAT MOMENT OF ENLIGHTENMENT.
WHAT THE LOVE WE ALL FELT COST.
MR. BRYSON...

...I KNOW WE'RE NOT SUPPOSED TO DISTURB YOU BUT YOUR BROTHER ACTIVATED THE INTRUDER ALARM.
MA'AM, WE'RE GOING TO HAVE TO ASK YOU TO LEAVE.
HUPP!
SO ASK.
OH, SNAP!
DON'T GET CUTE.
DON'T GET COCKY.
LIGHTS OUT, JOLTIN' JOE KATE-ZIER.
BOOM.

YIPE!
BRODE MY JAWR.
C'MERE--
STILL TWO OF 'EM--
LOST MY QUIVER BUT I CAN STILL USE THE BOW--
BATTER
UP--
FUTZ.
GRRRAH--
UH-OH--

AT THIS POINT IT BECOMES TWO GROWN MEN, ONE WITH A BROKEN JAW AND THE OTHER A BROKEN NOSE, STOMPING THE CRAP OUT OF A TEENAGE GIRL.
IT GOES AS WELL AS YOU'D THINK UNTIL--
--AWW.
THANK YOU, HIPPIE MAN.
THANK
MS. BISHOP.
THERE. SHE'S COMING TO. MS. BISHOP?
HOLD HER UP STRAIGHT, YOU GOON.
MS. BISHOP.
THANK YOU FOR REJOINING US, MS. BISHOP.

DIDJA...
DIDJA DO IT?

DID I DO WHAT, MS. BISHOP?

DID YOU STEAL YOUR BROTHER'S MUSIC AND LEAK IT ON THE INTERNET? TO SHAME HIM, OR EMBARRASS HIM, OR DRIVE HIM CRAZY ONCE AND FOR ALL?

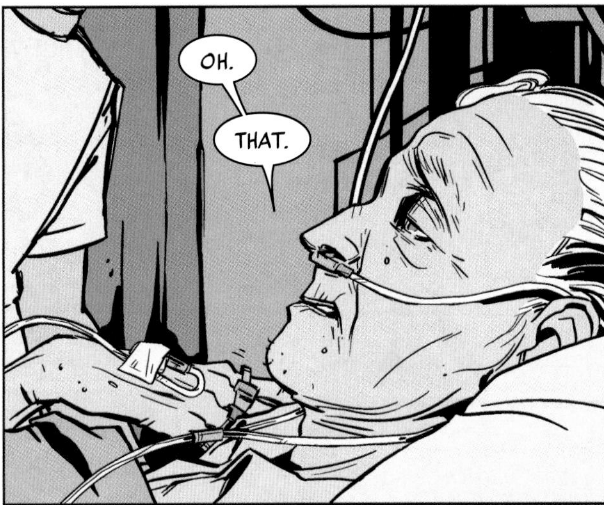
OH.
THAT.

OF COURSE I DID!

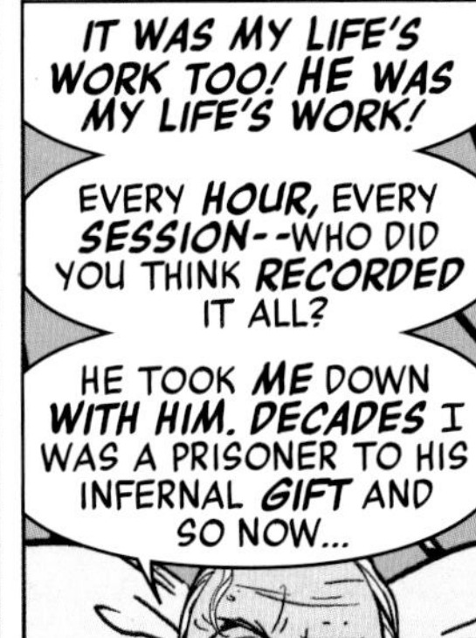
IT WAS MY LIFE'S WORK TOO! HE WAS MY LIFE'S WORK!
EVERY HOUR, EVERY SESSION--WHO DID YOU THINK RECORDED IT ALL?
HE TOOK ME DOWN WITH HIM. DECADES I WAS A PRISONER TO HIS INFERNAL GIFT AND SO NOW...

I'M TAKIN' HIM WITH ME, SWEETHEART.

I GOTTA GET THE HELL OUT OF LOS ANGELES.

AND YOU NEVER WENT BACK?
Thriftybuy

NOPE. I AM A TERRIBLE DETECTIVE.
IT WAS JUST TOO... THE TRAGEDY OF THOSE TWO GUYS, LOCKED IN THAT CRAZY HOUSE TOGETHER....
IT WAS TOO SAD. Y'KNOW?
BROTHERS ARE WEIRD.

AND BEING NUTS AND STONED ALL THE TIME AND RICHER THAN GOD CAN'T HELP MUCH EITHER.
YEAH, MY SISTER'S A REAL PARTY TOO...

WHAT IF I'M NOT CUT OUT FOR THIS?

WHAT, BEING A P.I.? TAKES TIME, KID, IS ALL. NOT EVERY CASE IS THE MALTESE FALCON.

I DON'T KNOW WHO THAT IS.
AND I KICK ASS BEING A P.I. ...

I MEAN, L.A.

PEOPLE CAN BE SO MEAN TO EACH OTHER AND OUT HERE YOU CAN TAKE BUS TOURS TO GET BETTER VIEWS OF IT ALL.
AW, THAT'S KID STUFF. THE FILTH HERE FLOATS, Y'SEE? DON'T LET IT SHAKE YOU.

KIND OF FEELS LIKE THAT GENIE'S ALREADY OUT OF THE BOTTLE.

SO MAKE A WISH.

50%

PERFORMING LIVE @ THE SANDBOX CLUB
WILL BRYSON
presents WISH
ONE NIGHT ONLY!

ARE YOU...
...FUTZING
KIDDING ME??

I DON'T BELIEVE IT.
I KNOW.
I DON'T BELIEVE IT.
I KNOW.

OKAY SO THIS NEXT ONE, YOU MIGHT HAVE HEARD IN YOUR E-MAIL OR HOWEVER THAT WORKS.
PARTS OF IT ANYWAY.

AND THERE SHOULD BE SOME TRUMPETS IN THE MIDDLE BUT YOU'LL GET THE IDEA.
IT'S CALLED "BABY I GOT NO TIME TO RUN," AND I'D LIKE TO DEDICATE IT TO TWO PEOPLE:

MY LATE BROTHER GREY, WHO WAS WITH ME EVERY STEP OF THE WAY IN MY LIFE AS AN ARTIST...

...AND TO MY FAVORITE SUPER HERO, WHO ALWAYS LOOKS SO GREAT IN PURPLE...

INCREDIBLE HULK, WHEREVER YOU ARE, THIS IS FOR YOU, BUDDY.

OH, SWEETIE--
--NO, NO, IT'S OKAY, I'M OKAY--

IT'S BEAUTIFUL.

AND FOR A SECOND EVERYTHING IS PERFECT. THE CLUB, MY FRIENDS, MY NEW TOWN.
AND THIS...SHEET OF SOUND POURING OVER ME.
EVERYTHING BAD IN THE WORLD JUST MELTS AWAY AND--
FOUND YOU.
--THE HELL?
SERIOUSLY, WHAT THE HELL WAS THAT?
KATE...?
IT'S OVER.
IT WAS GOOD FOR A SECOND BUT NOW I KNOW--
"GOOD" IS ALL OVER.

18

AND SO, FIRMLY ENSCONCED--
--ENSCONCED?--
--IN HER NEW LIFE AS A PUBLIC DETECTIVE, HAWKEYE LIVED HAPPILY EVER AFTER IN CALIFORNIA, FAR AWAY FROM NEW YORK JERKS AND NEEDY ABUSIVE BLACK HOLES OF CRIPPLED EMOTIONS.

THE END.

OH, AND HER STUPID SNOOTY CAT.

MAYBE I'LL NEVER LEAVE.
50
75

MAYBE EVERYTHING'LL SETTLE DOWN OUT HERE AND BECOME PERFECT. MAYBE--
COFFEE!
SALE
OUT
IN
YOU'RE WHAAAAAAAAT.

YEAH, KID. I'M BLOWIN' TOWN. TRYING TO ANYWAY. I THINK I GOT MY SHOT AND I'M GONNA TAKE IT.
BUT--
--I KNOW IT'S HAPPENING OUT OF THE BLUE--
YOU DID THE WHOLE THING, THE "STAY-IN-L.A.-THING"--
HEY, LOOK, KID...

THE BRASS RING COMES UP YOU GOTTA GRAB FOR IT. WINDOWS OF OPPORTUNITY.
ESCAPE VELOCITY. IT'S--
OKAY THOSE AREN'T EVEN COMPLETE SENTENCES.
KID...

YOU WANT A CAT?

SO I SAID, "WHAT'S THE WORST THAT CAN HAPPEN?!?"

OOH, GIRL, YOU MESSED UP.

THIS'LL BE COOL, RIGHT?
HE'LL STILL BE AROUND.
HE HASN'T LEFT TOWN YET AND I CAN GIVE HIM THIS HELLBEAST #$@&! OF A CAT BACK TO HIM.

SURE. WITH A LITTLE GOOD LUCK.
SUPER HEROES HAVE GOOD LUCK, RIGHT?

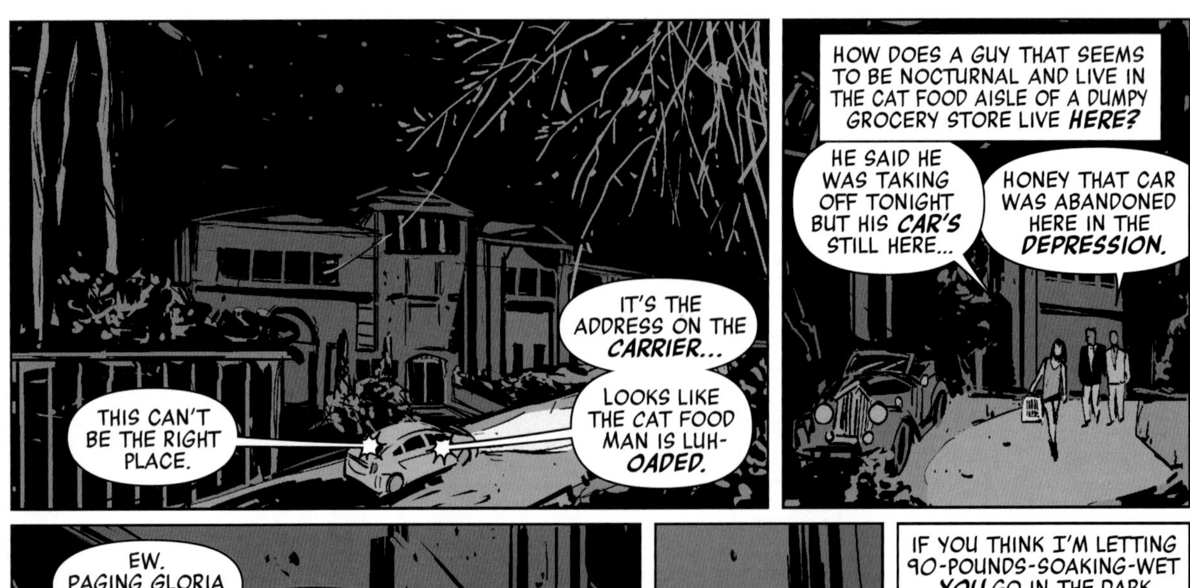
THIS CAN'T BE THE RIGHT PLACE.
IT'S THE ADDRESS ON THE CARRIER...
LOOKS LIKE THE CAT FOOD MAN IS LUH-OADED.
HOW DOES A GUY THAT SEEMS TO BE NOCTURNAL AND LIVE IN THE CAT FOOD AISLE OF A DUMPY GROCERY STORE LIVE HERE?
HE SAID HE WAS TAKING OFF TONIGHT BUT HIS CAR'S STILL HERE...
HONEY THAT CAR WAS ABANDONED HERE IN THE DEPRESSION.

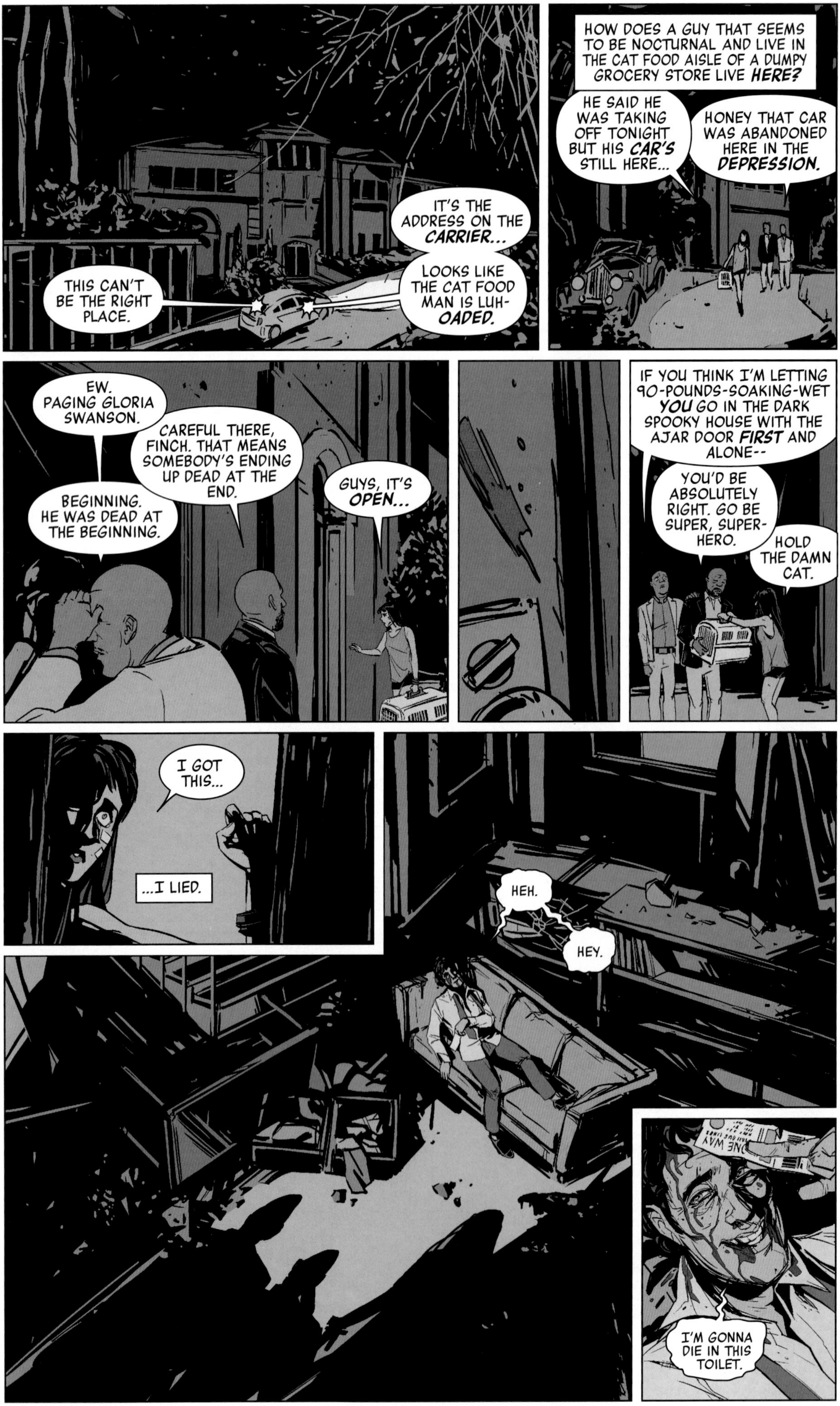

EW. PAGING GLORIA SWANSON.
CAREFUL THERE, FINCH. THAT MEANS SOMEBODY'S ENDING UP DEAD AT THE END.
BEGINNING. HE WAS DEAD AT THE BEGINNING.
GUYS, IT'S OPEN...
IF YOU THINK I'M LETTING 90-POUNDS-SOAKING-WET YOU GO IN THE DARK SPOOKY HOUSE WITH THE AJAR DOOR FIRST AND ALONE--
YOU'D BE ABSOLUTELY RIGHT. GO BE SUPER, SUPER-HERO.
HOLD THE DAMN CAT.

I GOT THIS...
...I LIED.
HEH.
HEY.
ONE WAY
I'M GONNA DIE IN THIS TOILET.

THEY TOLD ME I'D NEVER LEAVE L.A. ALIVE.

THAT WAS TWENTY-TWO YEARS AGO.

NOT A BAD RECORD IN THIS TOWN...
=KEFF=

OKAY, ONE-- WHO?

TWO, WHAT?

THREE, CAN WE KEEP YOUR CAT STILL?
WHO'S A GOOD CAT.

LOOK AT YOU.
=KEFF=
SO--

KAFFKAFFKARRFFKAFF

--SO OPTIMISTIC.
WHO'S KEEPING ME HERE? WHO ELSE...?

SUPER VILLAINS.

"IT WAS THE NINETIES.

"OUR SODAS WERE CRYSTAL.
"OUR T-SHIRTS WERE HYPERCOLOR.
"OUR HARD DRIVES WERE ALMOST 80 MEGS.
"AND I WAS A HACK WRITER SET LOOSE ON ALL THE WEIRD SECRETS LOS ANGELES HAD TO OFFER.
"THE WEIRD MURDER BEAT LED ME ALL OVER THE MAP, COVERING SPECTACLE AND MYSTERY WHEREVER I'D FIND IT. BODY HARVESTING...
"RAVES AND RAIDS ON AREA 51...
"THE BIRTH OF CYBERCRIME...
"EUROPEAN POP STARS...
CE LINE DO NOT CROSS
CROSS POLI
"...AND OTHER MONSTERS."
FUNNY THING, IT WASN'T THE WEIRD CRIME JOURNALISM THAT BROKE ME.
AFTER THE VAMPIRE STUFF, HOLLYWOOD CALLED. AND THAT...
"...IS A COMPLETELY DIFFERENT LOS ANGELES FREAK BEAT."

"IT WAS THE MONEY, THAT DID IT.
"MONEY RUINS EVERYTHING.
"IT RUINED ME..."

WHOA! SORRY, I--
DAMMIT, YOU STUPID VALLEY TRASH, I--

MY WORD-- HAROLD?
HIYAH, MR. HUDSON--DIDN'T KNOW YOU'D BE HERE.
PUBLISHERS ALWAYS LIVED IN A HIGHER TAX BRACKET THAN THEIR FREELANCE STRINGERS, EH? BUT NOW THAT YOU'VE GOT THOSE HOLLYWOOD MILLIONS...

I GUESS...I DON'T KNOW ANYONE HERE. I DON'T EVEN KNOW WHY I CAME...
YOU CAME BECAUSE WHEN COUNT LUCHINO NEFF AND HIS DAUGHTER GIA OPEN THEIR DOORS, YOU COME.

IF YOU SAY SO...BUT, MAN, HUD, JUST LOOK AT ME. EVERYONE HERE IS SO YOUNG AND BEAUTIFUL AND... Y'KNOW, FIT. HAPPY.
I MEAN, I DO A LOT OF WALKING AND CARDIO, THESE PEOPLE ALL LOOK LIKE THEY WERE CARVED IN A GYM...
HA HA, YES, THAT...

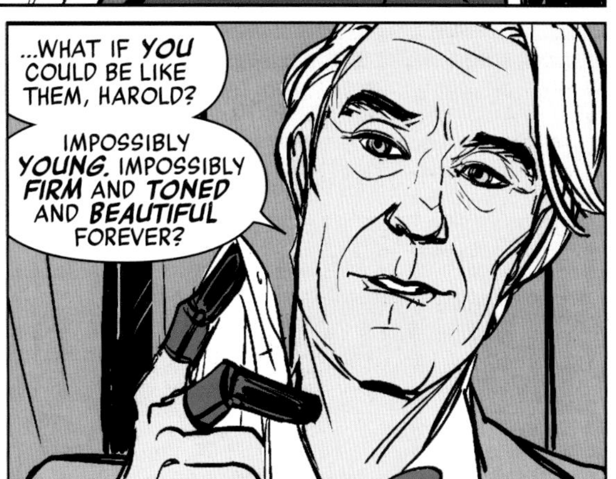
...WHAT IF YOU COULD BE LIKE THEM, HAROLD?
IMPOSSIBLY YOUNG. IMPOSSIBLY FIRM AND TONED AND BEAUTIFUL FOREVER?

THEN I SUPPOSE I WOULDN'T HAVE SPENT SENIOR PROM PLAYING DUNGEONS AND DRAGONS...
"WHAT THE HELL WAS HE TALKING ABOUT?
"PLASTIC SURGERY? BOTOX?
"IT FELT LIKE ANOTHER MYSTERIOUS INITIATION I DIDN'T UNDERSTAND. AND I NEVER GOT THE CHANCE TO ASK.
"PETER HUDSON, MY ONE-TIME PUBLISHER, DIED A FEW DAYS LATER IN A CAR CRASH.

"BEING RICH MEANS THAT YOU CAN HAVE THE RIGHT KIND OF PAPER CUPS SENT TO ME FROM THE CITY.
"COFFEE DOESN'T TASTE RIGHT ANY OTHER WAY.

"SO THE MORNING I READ ABOUT PETER HUDSON'S DEATH IN THE PAPER, I'M SITTING ON THE BEACH DRINKING MY L.A. COFFEE FROM AN N.Y. CUP...
"AND I SEE HIS 26-YEAR-OLD GHOST GO JOGGING BY.

"IT WAS HUD.
"I SWEAR TO GOD. I TRIED TO MAKE A SOUND...
HUHHH...?
"AND HE HEARD ME.

"HE TURNED AWAY AND RAN FASTER. THE WOMAN KEPT PERFECT PACE WITH HIM.
"I SWEAR TO GOD, THEY WEREN'T EVEN SWEATING...

"I MIGHT HAVE BEEN DONE WITH THE FREAK BEAT, BUT THE FREAK BEAT WASN'T DONE WITH ME.

"HUD DIED WHEN HE RAMMED THE BACK OF A SEMI. BOTH CARS EXPLODED.
"THE SEMI DRIVER WAS 'BURNED BEYOND RECOGNITION'.
"THAT SEEMED WEIRD.
"WHY WOULDN'T NEFF INTERSTATE TRUCKLINES KNOW WHO WAS DRIVING THEIR TRUCKS?

"AND SO FOR THE SECOND TIME IN A WEEK, THE NAMES HUDSON AND NEFF CROSSED MY PATH SEEMINGLY AT RANDOM.
"I WAS ABLE TO CASH IN A COUPLE FAVORS FROM A FRIEND AT THE L.A.P.D. FROM MY DAYS ON THE BEAT.
SHAKE.
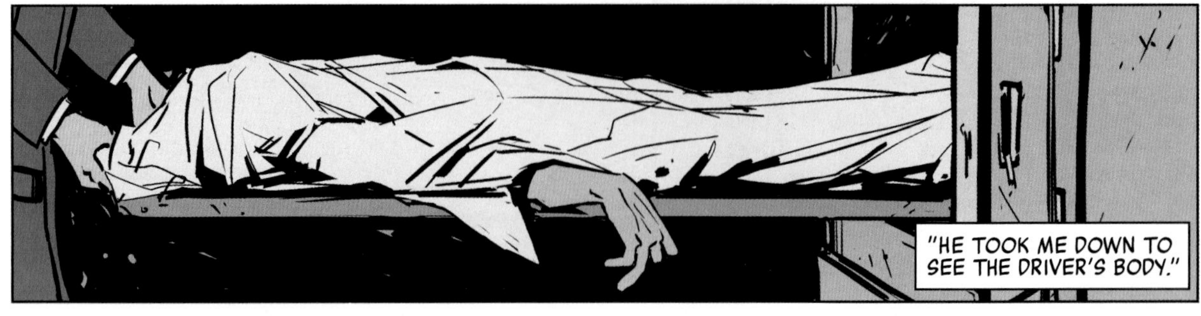
"HE TOOK ME DOWN TO SEE THE DRIVER'S BODY."

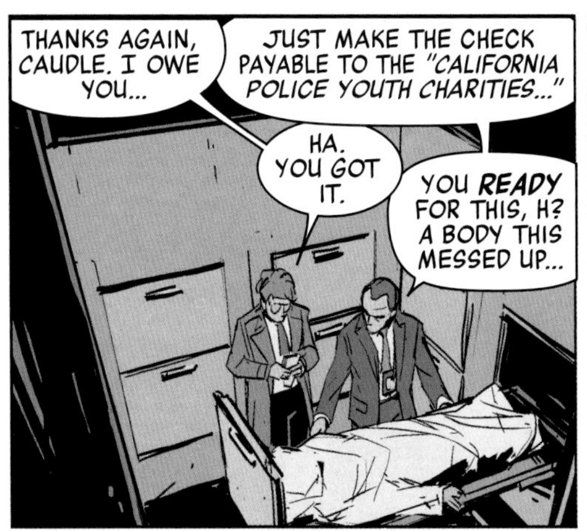
THANKS AGAIN, CAUDLE. I OWE YOU...
JUST MAKE THE CHECK PAYABLE TO THE "CALIFORNIA POLICE YOUTH CHARITIES..."
HA. YOU GOT IT.
YOU READY FOR THIS, H? A BODY THIS MESSED UP...

...YOU CAN'T EVER UNSEE IT.

"HE WAS RIGHT. I WAS--I AM--
"--HAUNTED BY WHAT WAS DONE TO THAT BODY.
"IT WASN'T A CAR CRASH.
"IT WAS VIVISECTION.

"I WENT BACK TO THE NEFF'S.

"I BROUGHT THE EXOTIC TOOLS OF MY TRADE...

"AND THE MORE TRADITIONAL.

"I WAS ARMED TO THE TEETH.

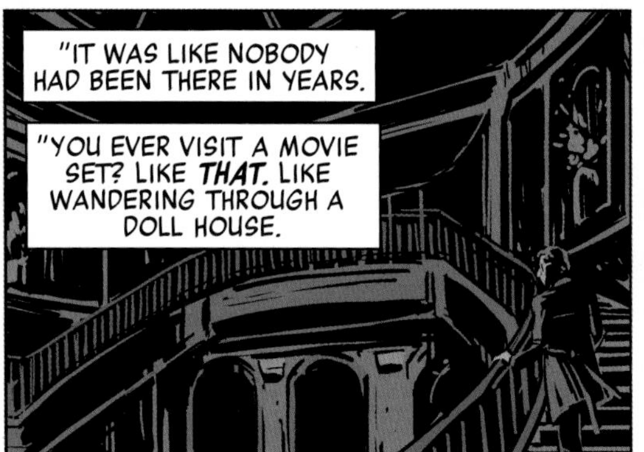
"IT WAS LIKE NOBODY HAD BEEN THERE IN YEARS.
"YOU EVER VISIT A MOVIE SET? LIKE THAT. LIKE WANDERING THROUGH A DOLL HOUSE.

"EVERY ROOM HAD MORE NOTHING SO I KEPT HUNTING.

"FOR SOMETHING. FOR ANYTHING.
"AND THEN I FOUND IT AND MY LIFE WAS PRETTY MUCH OVER."
WHAT.
WHAT DID YOU FIND?

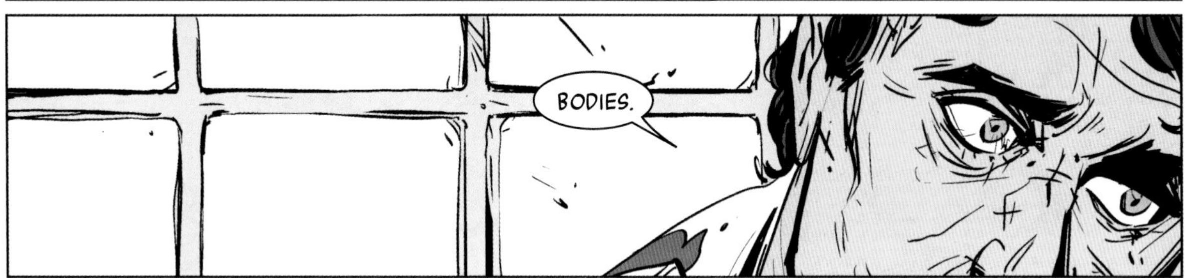
BODIES.

THEY WERE DOING SOMETHING WITH BODIES...
"NEFF AND THAT WEIRD DAUGHTER OF HIS.
"RUMORS ON THE DARKNETS PEGGED THEM AS A DADDY-DAUGHTER SUPER-VILLAIN TEAM BUT WHO KNOWS.
"THEY WERE GHOULS. MONSTERS. THEY WERE TRYING TO...
"THEY HAD BODY PARTS AND MACHINERY AND THEY...IT LOOKED LIKE THEY WERE TRYING SOME REAL FRANKENSTEIN STUFF DOWN THERE.
"IT WAS LIKE THEY WERE TRYING TO MAKE COPIES.
"I DROVE LIKE HELL. GOODBYE L.A., GOODBYE HOUSE, GOODBYE MONEY--
"OF COURSE THEY FOLLOWED. I WAS ALREADY TRAPPED AND I DIDN'T KNOW IT.
"THEY FORCED ME OFF THE ROAD. THE JALOPY ROLLED SIX TIMES BEFORE I BLACKED OUT.
"I CAME TO AND THEY WERE BEATING THE HELL OUT OF ME."
THEY TOLD ME I WASN'T ALLOWED TO LEAVE LOS ANGELES.
AND EVERY TIME I'VE TRIED SINCE THEY SOMEHOW FIND ME, STOP ME, AND BEAT ME UP ALL OVER AGAIN.
WHO, "NEFF"?
"HIS GOONS.
"THE MEN IN BLACK."

UM.

GO AHEAD, LAUGH.
I'M STILL NEVER GETTING OUT OF THIS TOWN ALIVE...
"IS HE RIGHT?"

SOMEBODY BEAT HIM UP.
AND HE CLEARLY THINKS HE'S RIGHT. WHO ARE WE TO SAY?
NEFF...THAT COULD BE SHORT FOR NEFARIA.
THAT THE ONE WITH THE LION AND TILDA SWINTON AND SUCH?
NEFARIA.

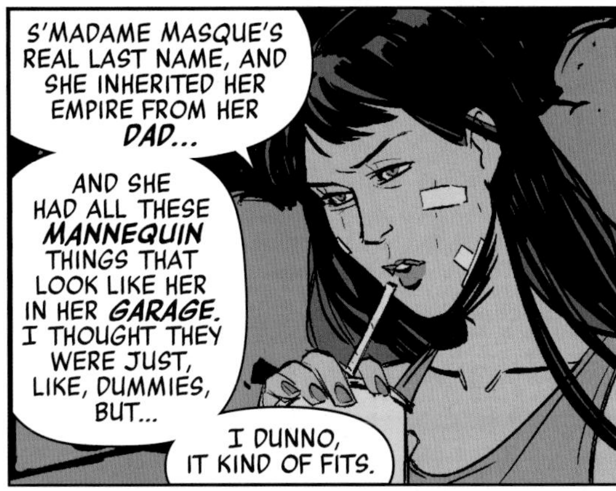
S'MADAME MASQUE'S REAL LAST NAME, AND SHE INHERITED HER EMPIRE FROM HER DAD...
AND SHE HAD ALL THESE MANNEQUIN THINGS THAT LOOK LIKE HER IN HER GARAGE. I THOUGHT THEY WERE JUST, LIKE, DUMMIES, BUT...
I DUNNO, IT KIND OF FITS.

IF CAT FOOD MAN REALLY KNOWS WHAT HE'S TALKING ABOUT, THE WOMAN THAT'S BEEN TRYING TO RUIN MY LIFE RUINED HIS, TOO.
WAIT UNTIL I TELL YOU ABOUT THE CRAZY WOMAN THAT'S BEEN TRYING TO RUIN OUR LIVES.
FINCH. BE NICE.

WHAT IF MADAME MASQUE IS THE REASON WHY EVERYTHING IN L.A. SUCKS?

L.A. OR JUST THE VALLEY?

YOU DID NOT JUST CALL "THE VALLEY" PART OF L.A.

HIS NAME IS "HAROLD H. HAROLD."
NO IT IS NOT.

YEP. I BOUGHT HIM THE TICKET, HE SHOWED ME HIS I.D.
"HAROLD H. HAROLD."
WELL WHAT DOES THE "H" STAND FOR...?

HAROLD.
ANYTHING DOING DOWN THERE?

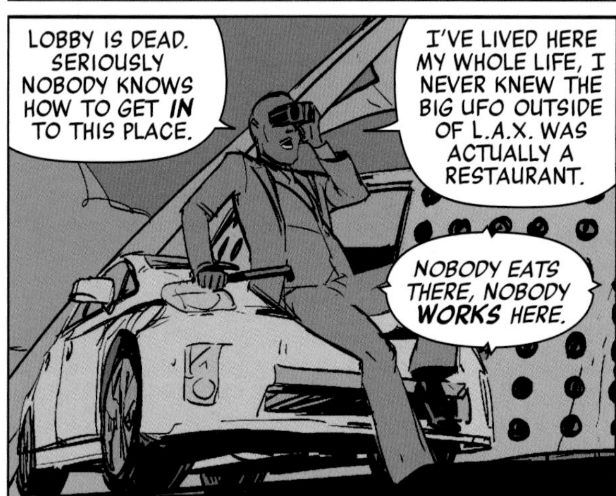
LOBBY IS DEAD. SERIOUSLY NOBODY KNOWS HOW TO GET IN TO THIS PLACE.
I'VE LIVED HERE MY WHOLE LIFE, I NEVER KNEW THE BIG UFO OUTSIDE OF L.A.X. WAS ACTUALLY A RESTAURANT.
NOBODY EATS THERE, NOBODY WORKS HERE.

WHAT KIND OF RESTAURANT DOESN'T HAVE TRASH TO TAKE OUT AT LEAST EVERY HALF-HOUR?
RIDICULOUS.
JUST KEEP YOUR EYES PEELED.

WE GOT TWO HOURS UNTIL MR. HAROLD H. HAROLD GOES WHEELS UP AND FINALLY GETS OUT OF L.A....
YO, CAN I HELP YOU?

JUST CHECKING TO SEE IF YOU WERE READY TO ORDER YET, OR...
I SAID I NEEDED A MINUTE WITH THE MENU AND THAT MEANS I NEED A MINUTE.
...BUT IT'S BEEN FIFTEEN...

SIR.
WEED?

BEG PARDON?
WHAT IS THIS, 1973?

ON THE CONTRARY, IT'S NEARLY 2013 I BELIEVE. AND IT'S **LEGAL** IF YOU HAVE THE RIGHT PAPER.
WELL I HAVE THE RIGHT PAPER... AND I HAVE THE RIGHT **PAPER,** IF YOU INTUIT MY DOUBLE-MEANING.
WOULD YOU LIKE TO GET A LITTLE HIGH BEFORE YOU FLY? I CAN ARRANGE SUCH.

AS A LIFESTYLE THING, IT'S OKAY BY ME, BUT NO THANK YOU.

NEED TO STAY SHARP.
GOT THE WHOLE REST OF MY LIFE AHEAD OF ME TODAY.

THAT'S TOO BAD.
I'M NOT LONG OUT OF **PRISON** AND LOOKING TO **EARN.**

SNAP.

HEY, WHAT THE--?
FLYNT WARD THE WEED LORD?!?

AWAY WITH HIM.
WE'VE A SCHEDULE TO KEEP...
YOU GOT IT, BOSS.
SURE THING, BOSS.
EXIT

THEY HEISENBERGED US!

WARD!
WE'RE NOT DONE.
I THINK WE ARE.

HAWKEYE.
FLATTERY WILL GET Y--

YYYYOW!

DON'T FOLLOW US.
WE ARE NOT IN THE MOOD.
EXIT

FRONT DOOR!
FRONT DOOR! THEY'RE

GONNA COME RIGHT OUT FRONT--
STOP YELLING--

OLD GUY'S GOT SURPRISINGLY STRONG LEGS--
MUST DO A LOT OF WALKING AND CARDIO--
--GGRRRAAAHH--

I WARNED YOU!
--AND THANKS FOR THE HEAD'S UP--
BIG MISTAKE--
EXIT
WAIT, I KNOW YOU, WEREN'T YOU THE GUY--
--HHHRRGK--
BOSS--
BOSS?
BOSS!
WHEN I PUT YOU ON ICE YOU STAY--
--DOWN!
THE HELL THEY ARE.
KATE, THEY'RE GETTING AWAY--

HEY!
GET BACK HERE WITH THAT INCAPACITATED OLD MAN!
HIS CAT HAS SPECIAL NEEDS!

MARCUS--
--I'M FINE JUST GO--

AWW, VAN.

DUM-DUM-DUM-DUMMMMM!

NOW JUST IMAGINE HOW GREAT THAT WOULD SOUND IF WE'D HAVE SPRUNG FOR THE DIGITAL CAR HORN.
GET IN.

STEADY--
--STEADY--

ARE YOU INSANE?
THAT SHOT IS IMPOSSIBLE AND COMPLETELY RECKLESS.

RELAX, MARCUS.

SAW A FRIEND OF MINE DO THIS ONCE--

TOURISTS!!

MOM!!
WHOA WHOA WHOA--

LAX
DAMMIT!

...DAMMIT.

I WANT TO BOTH PUNCH AND SPANK YOU AND I'D DO IT IF IT WASN'T POLICE BRUTALITY AND SEXUAL HARASSMENT.
WHAT COULD YOU POSSIBLY SAY THAT WOULD MAKE ME FEEL ANY DIFFERENT?

"HAROLD H. HAROLD"?
HE USED TO BE A CRIME WRITER? AND MAYBE, LIKE--WROTE ABOUT WEIRD CRIMES?
THINK HE WAS A FRIEND.

THAT IS--
THAT'S LITERALLY JUST ABOUT THE ONLY THING THAT COULD'VE COME OUT OF YOUR MOUTH THAT MAKES ME NOT WANT TO MURDER YOU, Y'KNOW THAT?

HAVEN'T HEARD FROM HIM IN YEARS. HOW IS HE?
TRAPPED IN L.A., OR SO HE CLAIMED. HE ASKED ME TO TAKE CARE OF HIS CAT, WHO IS, LIKE, THE HITLER OF CATS--
--THEN I FOUND HIM ALL BEAT UP AND SAYING THERE WAS A CONSPIRACY TO KEEP HIM HERE.
I BOUGHT HIM A TICKET TO PHOENIX AND DROVE HIM TO L.A.X. MYSELF TO PUT HIM ON THE PLANE...

WHO ARE THE NEFFS?
ARE THEY THE NEFARIAS?

KID, YOU ARE, SERIOUSLY, AMAZING.
IF I WORKED IN INSURANCE I'D FOLLOW YOU AROUND ALL DAY AND DOUBLE THE POLICY RATES FOR EVERYONE YOU SPOKE TO...

...YEAH?
WHAT.
PARDON ME, DETECTIVE CAUDLE--
...THERE'S BEEN A BODY FOUND WE NEED YOU TAKE LEAD ON?
YEAH.

KATE...
GO HOME.
YOU MIGHT'VE FINALLY CAUGHT THE WRONG TIGER BY THE TOE HERE.

OH, HERE, MA'AM, YOUR FRIEND LEFT THIS FOR YOU.
SHE SAID SHE COULDN'T HANG AROUND ANYMORE BUT WOULD SEE HER BACK HOME...
WHO?

MY DEAREST KATE...

WE CAN ALL BE HAPPY FOR OUR DEAR FRIEND MR. HAROLD H. HAROLD, LATE OF THE HOLLYWOOD HILLS.

HE FINALLY FOUND HIS WAY OUT OF LOS ANGELES, WITH YOUR HELP, OF COURSE.

AND SO NOW I FIND MYSELF LESS ONE PLAYMATE, LESS ONE GAME TO WHILE AWAY THE IDLE HOURS. OR SO I THOUGHT, HAWKEYE.

NOW YOU AND HE HAVE SOMETHING IN COMMON. THE ONLY WAY YOU'LL LEAVE THIS TOWN IS IN A BODY BAG.
MM

AND REPEATING OUR TOP STORY AT THIS HOUR...
OH, I DON'T KNOW, MAYBE IT'S NOT SO BAD OUT HERE AFTER ALL...

A BODY WAS FOUND IN A GRISLY CRIME SCENE ATOP--
I MEAN YOU CAN'T BEAT THE WEATHER...
STUPID PHONE.

I SWEAR YOU NEED TO HAVE GIRLY LITTLE FINGERS TO HIT ALL THESE TINY LITTLE KEYS.
THIS PHONE IS THE WORST.

AH! HERE WE GO.
CONTACTS... OH. OH, NO, WAIT THAT'S--
OKAY. HERE. HERE... UH...
KATE?

WAS ANY OF THAT A SINGLE TRAIN OF THOUGHT?

I LIFTED WARD'S PHONE WHEN WE FOUGHT. SEE? "WEED LORD."
FIGURED THERE'D BE SOME PRIMO DATA WE COULD USE ON IT.

ESPECIALLY IF HE'S TIED IN WITH NEFF-SLASH-NEFARIA AND KEEPS...
KEEPS HIS...
OH, GOD.

THEY'RE GOING TO TRY AND KILL CLINT BARTON.

THERE'S AN EMAIL HERE THAT AUTHORIZES IT. IT'S LIKE A SUPER VILLAIN A.P.B.
OH, CLINT.
WHAT DID YOU DO?

I GOTTA GET OUT OF LOS ANGELES, FINCH.
I GOTTA GO HOME.

KATIE, DARLING...

THIS WAS HOME.

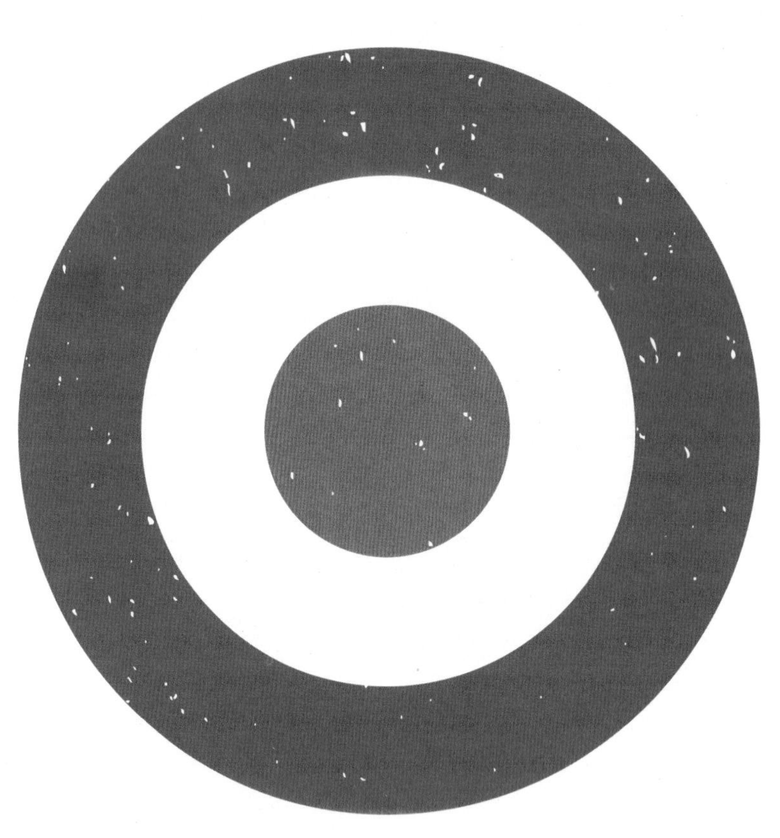

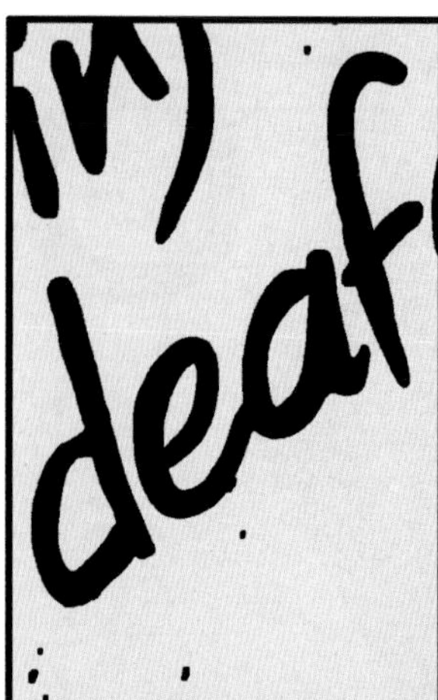
in)
deaf

midd
damaged.
the injury
been deafened
lly and I hope
mporarily

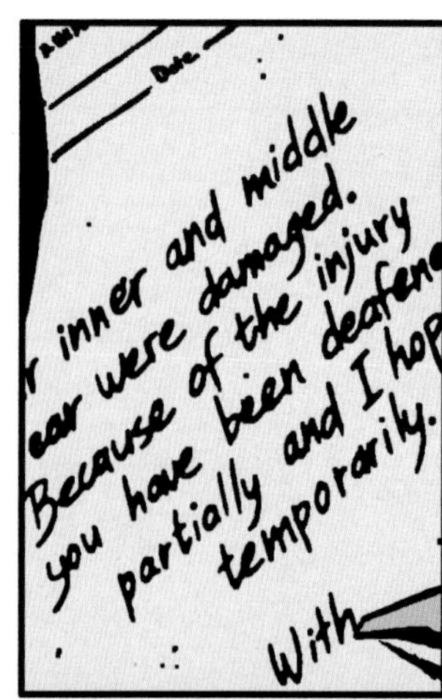
Date
r inner and middle
ear were damaged.
Because of the injury
you have been deafene
partially and I hop
temporarily.
With

Date
r inner and middle
ear were damaged.
Because of the injury
you have been deafened
partially and I hope
temporarily.
With care and
DR.

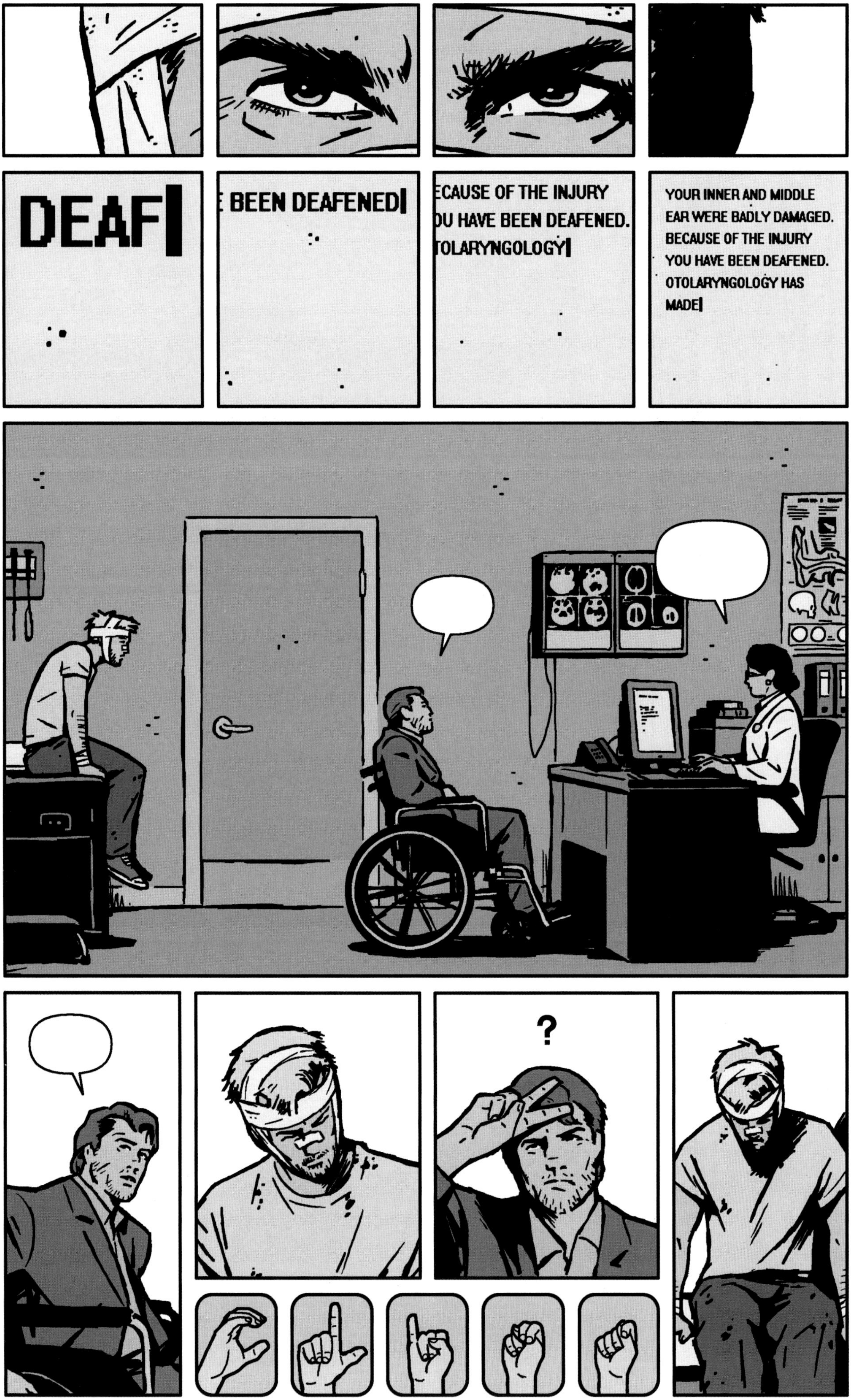

ECAUSE OF THE INJURY
OU HAVE BEEN DEAFENED.
TOLARYNGOLOGY

YOUR INNER AND MIDDLE
EAR WERE BADLY DAMAGED.
BECAUSE OF THE INJURY
YOU HAVE BEEN DEAFENED.
OTOLARYNGOLOGY HAS
MADE

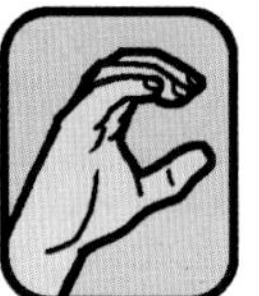

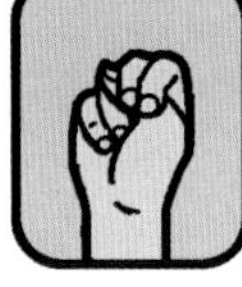
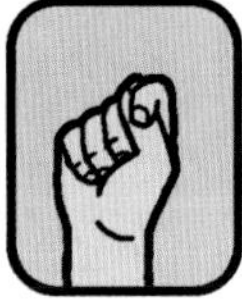

HOSPITAL
7048

1

3
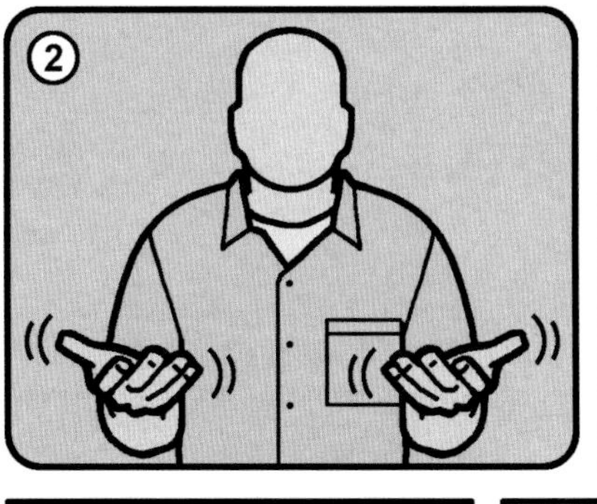
2
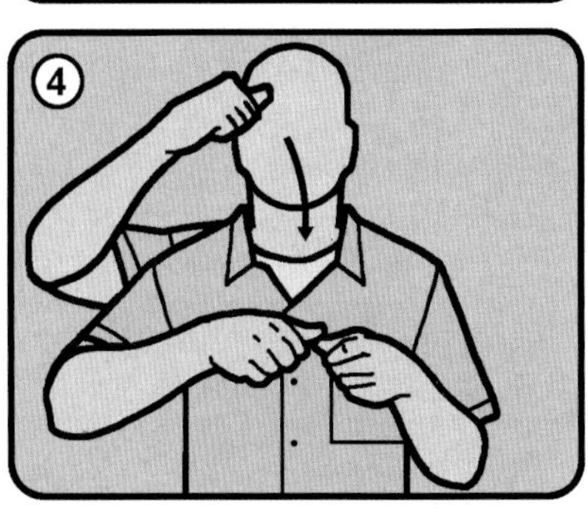
4

"IS...

"IS MEANING...
'ALLIGATORS'?"
"BRO, I GOTS NO IDEA WHAT SIGN MEANS THAT."

Arrivals
PSH. THESE TWO BROS.

WHY THERE BE ALLIGATORS AT AIRPORT, BRO? YOU STUPID, BRO.
IS WOLVES ZONE.
ИВАН

YOU NEED SIGN FOR ME?

TAKE CRAP.
WHERE LIMO?
OUT FRONT, BOSS.

WHOA, BRO.
CLASSY RIDE, BROS! WHAT IS THIS...

IVAN'S FUNERAL--?

WELCOME BACK, IVAN.

I, UH.
THANK YOU? THANK YOU, SIR?

NO.

NO, NO, NO--

IVAN.

TAKE IT.

IS...
...WHAT IS THIS FOR?

WHY DO YOU THINK WE BROUGHT YOU BACK?
YOU HAVE A RAT PROBLEM THAT NEEDS FIXING--

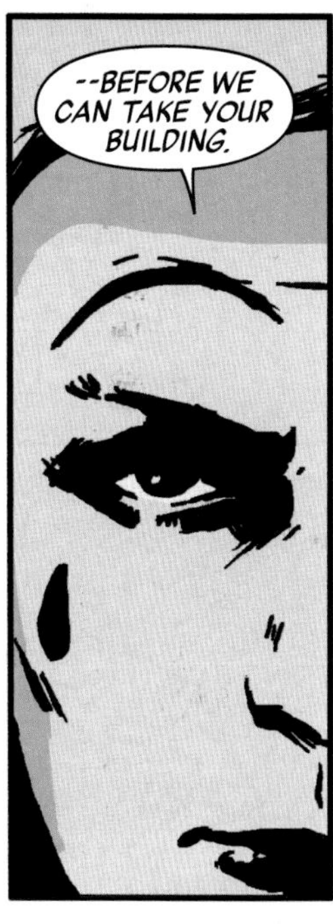
--BEFORE WE CAN TAKE YOUR BUILDING.

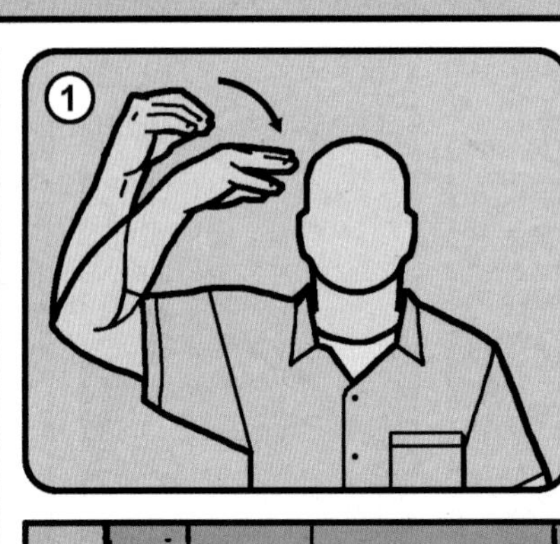

2

3

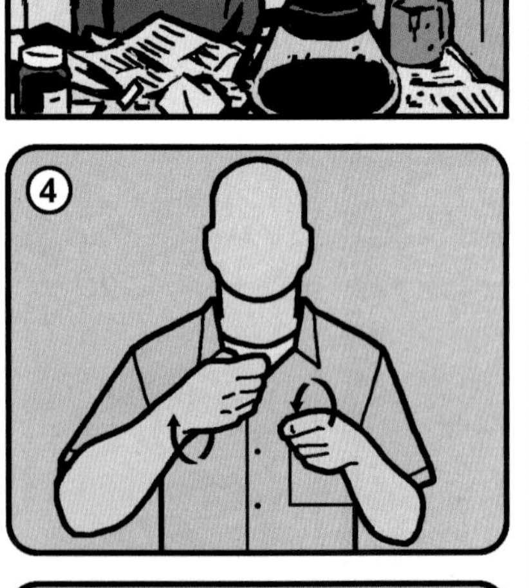

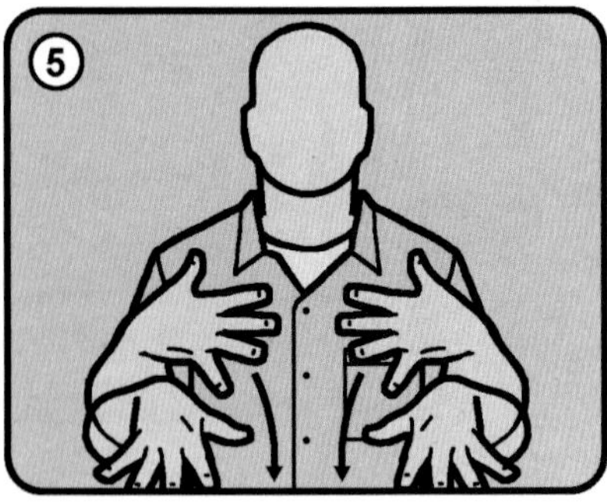

?

H
STUPID
STUBBORN-ASS...

ASS!

WAS THAT YOU I JUST HEARD HOLLERING THE A-WORD IN MY HALLWAY?
NO, S'WAS A...
UH...
IT WAS A...
YEAH, IT WAS ME, SORRY.
UNCLE BARNEY!
UNCLE BARNEY!

HEY, KIDS.

HEYAH, HERO. HOW'S YOUR BOO-BOOS?
AND HOW IS *HE* TODAY?

HE IS AS *"CLINT BARTON"* AS CLINT BARTON'S EVER BEEN.
WON'T SPEAK, WON'T SIGN...S'LIKE WHEN WE WERE KIDS. HE'S ***EMBARRASSED*** AND GOT TOO MUCH PRIDE TO ASK FOR--

--HE'S A PAIN IN THE A-WORD. THE KING OF A-WORDS.
AHH, CRAP.

1
...
?
2
3

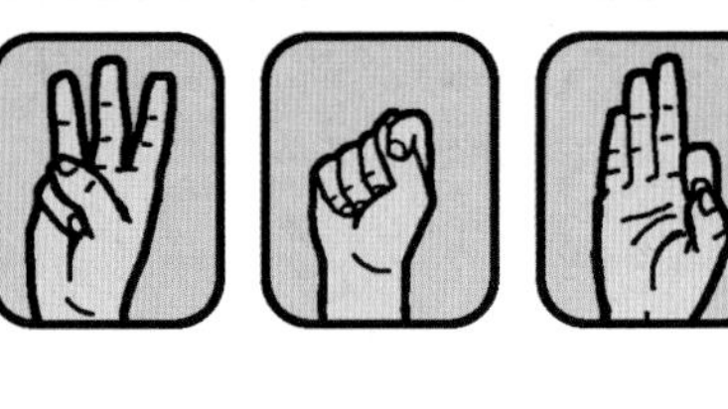

(something)
NOT MUTE.
YOU'RE
DEA(F)(?)

(Clint...)

(...Okay?)

(that son of a b(ench)?)

2

1

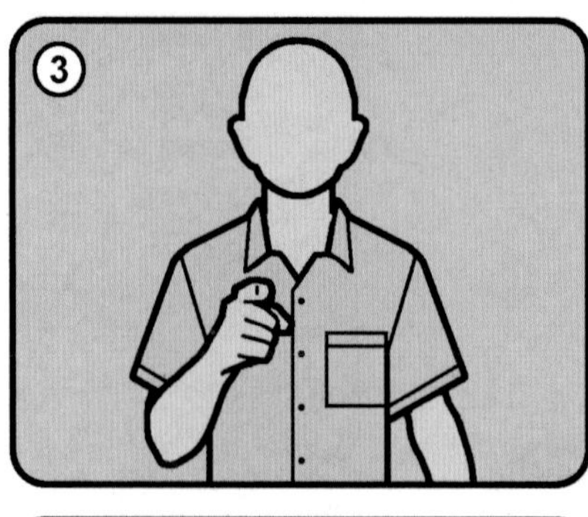
3
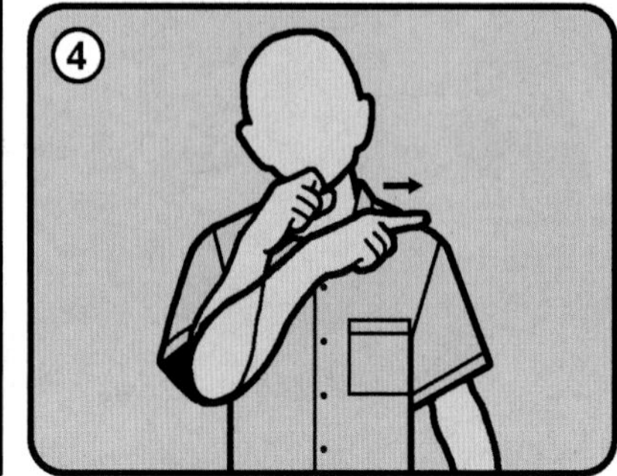
4

(something get(?) up Clint)

1

2

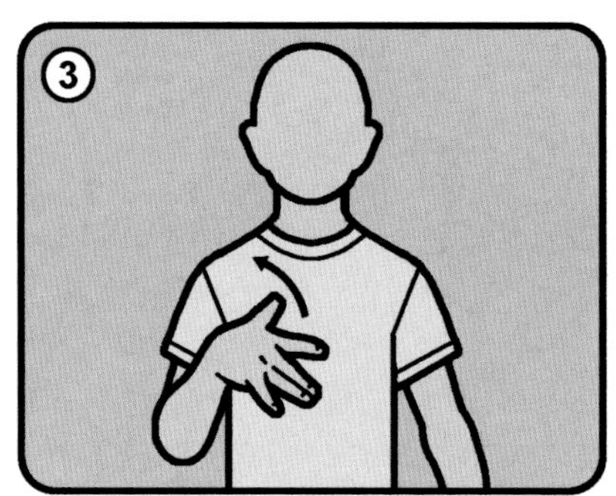
3

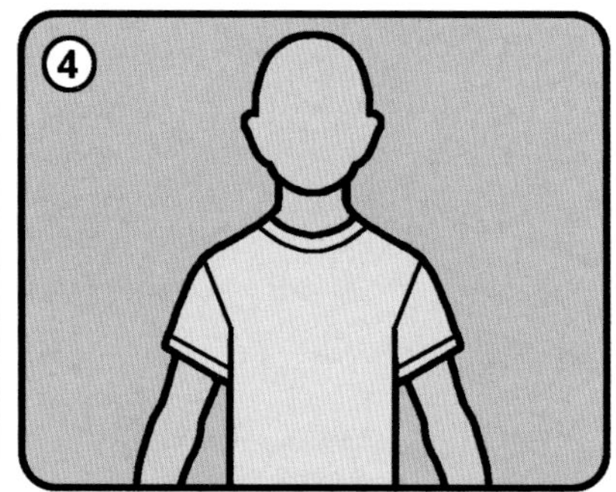
4

I CAN'T.

(GET UP!)

RRAAAAAA

(LOOK AT ME.)
(Make everything something to HIT WITH.)
(AND HIT THEM UNTIL THEY STOP.)

1
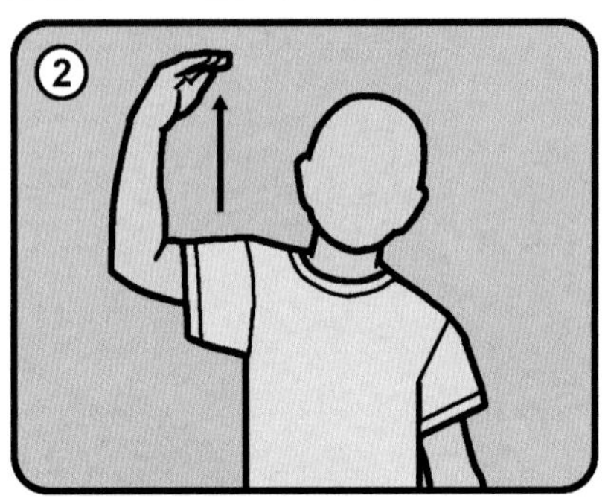
2

3

4
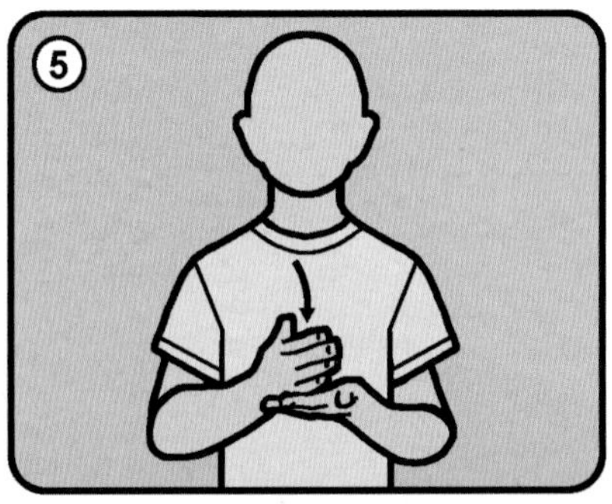
5

6

(Then we OUTLAST him)
(UNDERSTAND?)

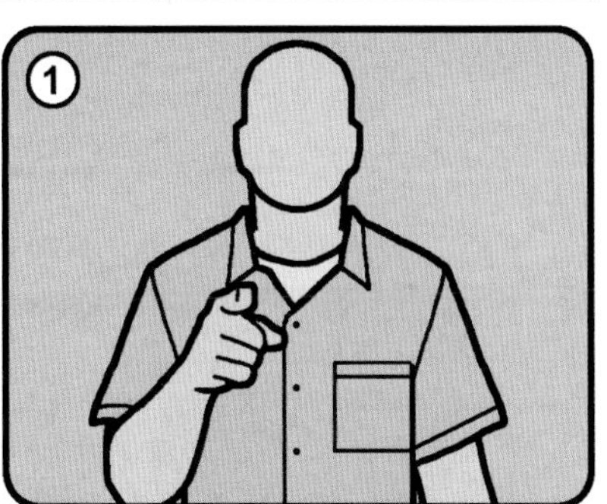

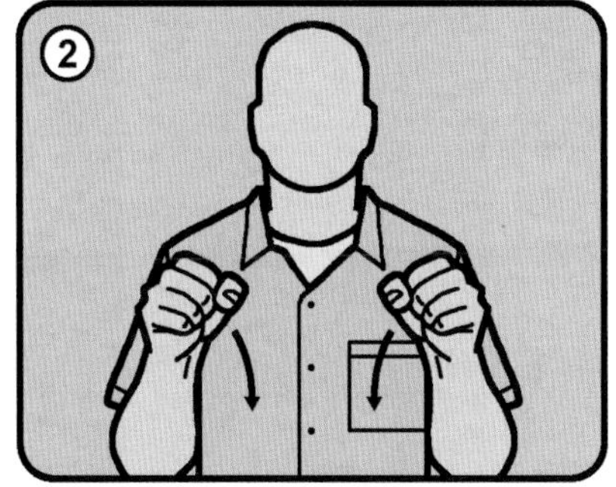

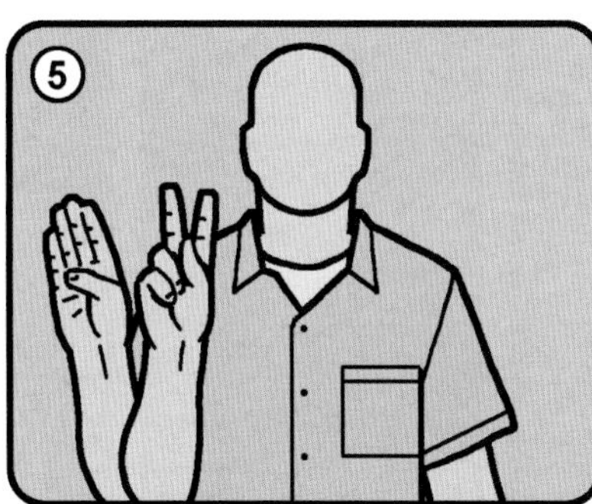

(I know you('re?) lip reading)

(you can get it back)

(look at ME)

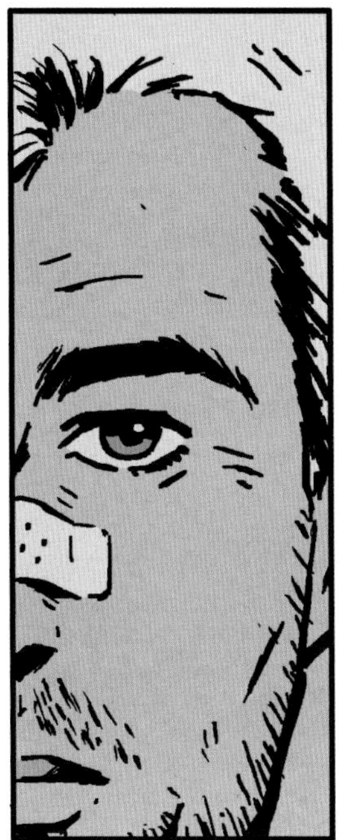

AND SO I SAID TO THOSE GUYS I SAID--
"OKAY-- TOUGH GUYS..."

"YOU GUYS AIN'T SO TOUGH!" AND THEN GUESS WHAT I SAID.
G'ON. GUESS.
GUESS.

"IT'S CLOBBERIN' TIME."

THAT'S RIGHT. THAT'S EXACTLY WHAT I SAID. SO THEN I SAID, KIDS, I SAID--
KNOK KNOK
WHO COULD THAT BE?

NOW, LOOK: ANYBODY CAN GET IN A FIGHT. ME, YOU, YOUR MOMS, ANYONE.
FIGHTIN'S EASY. FIGHTIN'S JUST A THING YOU DO. YOU HIT AND...

YOU GET HIT AND THE ONE THAT CAN HURT AND GET HURT THE MOST THE LONGEST WINS.
EVEN DUMB OL' UNCLE BARNEY CAN DO THAT.

BUT TO ACTUALLY DO GOOD, Y'SEE.
TO DO GOOD--
--YA GOTTA BE GOOD. YA GOTTA--

1

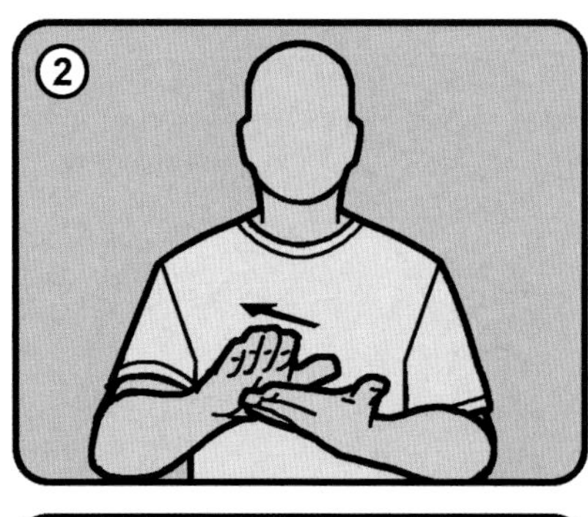
2

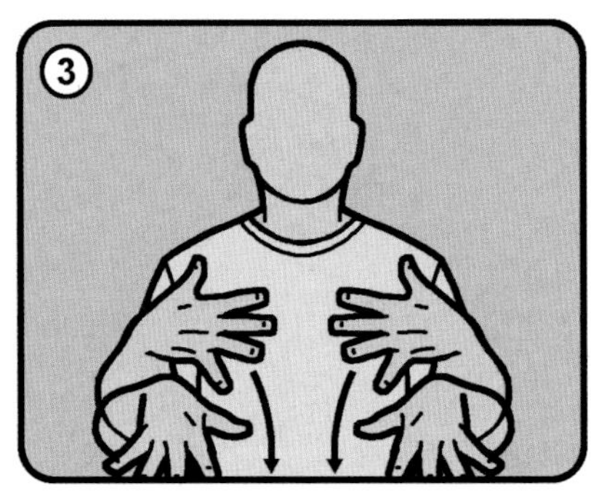
3

4

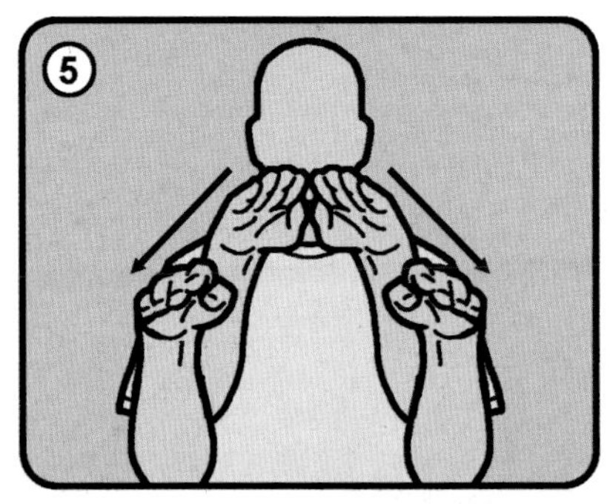
5

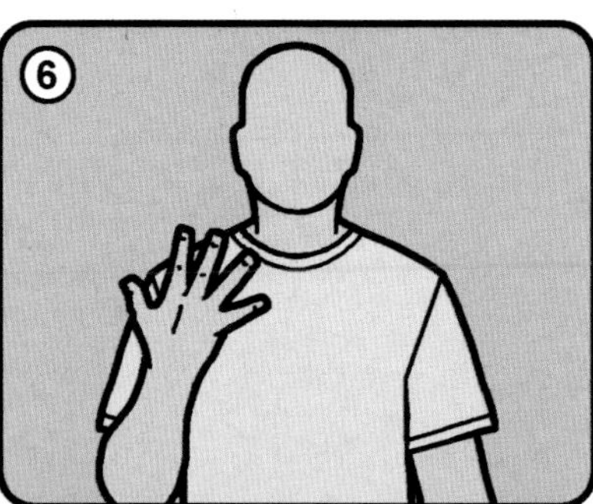
6

(Everybody- everybody, rooftop, five minutes)
(got it)
(y'freakin' fancy lad)

HEY, SO, UH.
I'M DEAF.
THEY DEAFENED ME.
I'M DEAF AND WE NEED TO TALK. SO...
SO I'M GONNA SIGN WHAT I HAVE TO SAY.
I NEED THE PRACTICE AND I'M NOT GONNA HIDE ANYMORE.
BARNEY'LL TRANSLATE. IT'LL BE OKAY.
OKAY? OKAY.

1
2
3
4
5
6
7
('you will stop them'... HOW?)

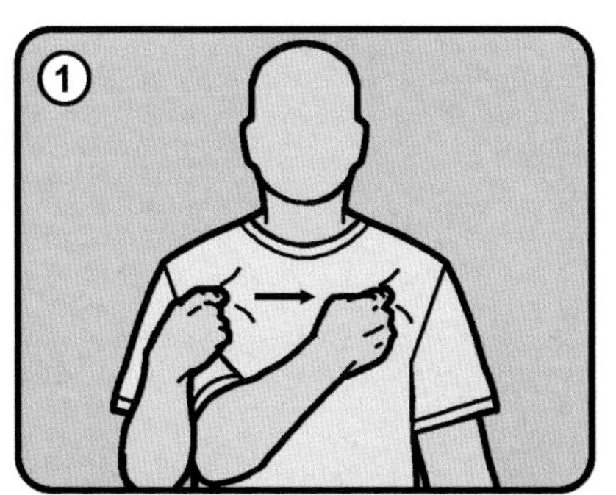
1

("We"?)

WE.

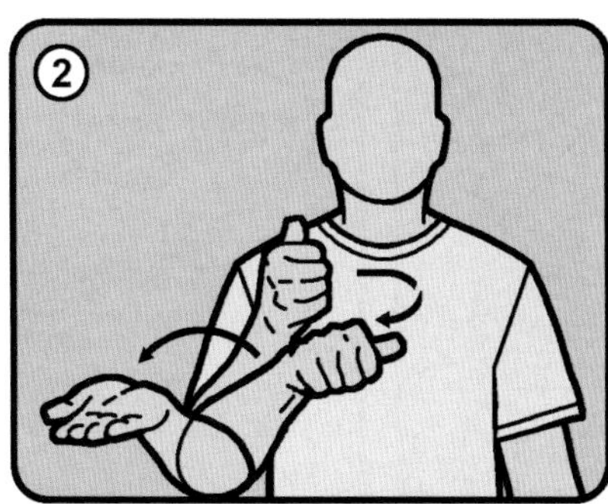
2
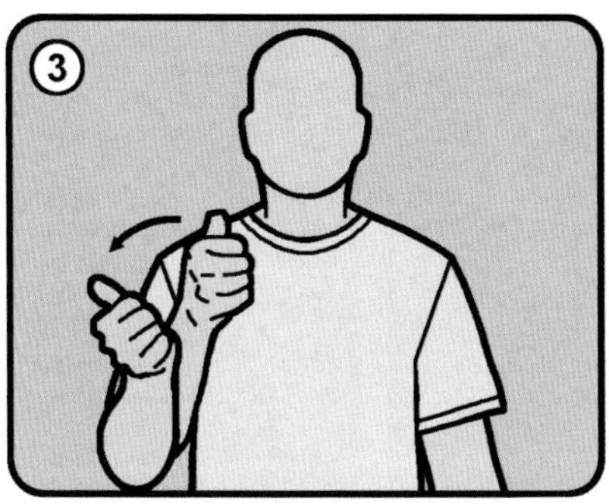
3

(you ain't done YET)
(one more thing)
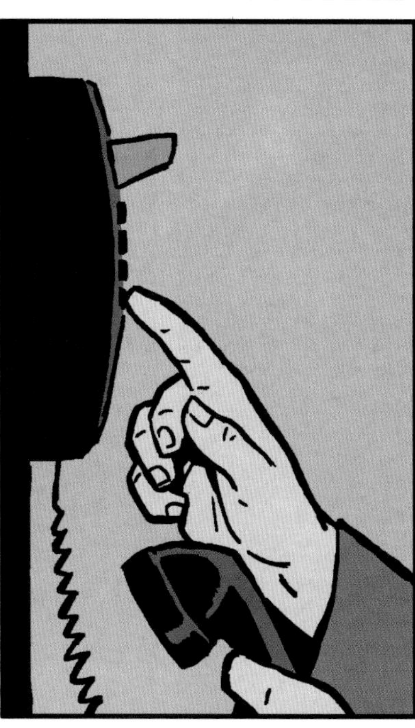

БОЛВАНЫ TOWN
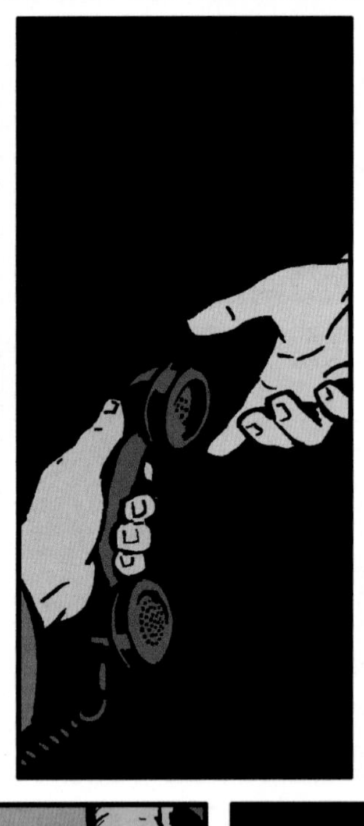

JESS?
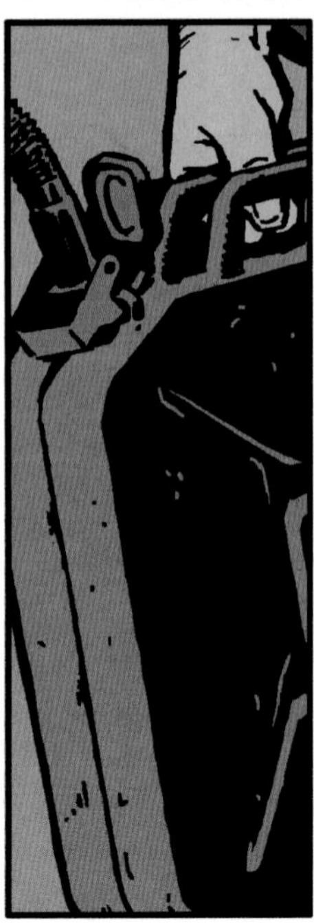

I'M **SORRY** AND I NEED YOUR HELP.
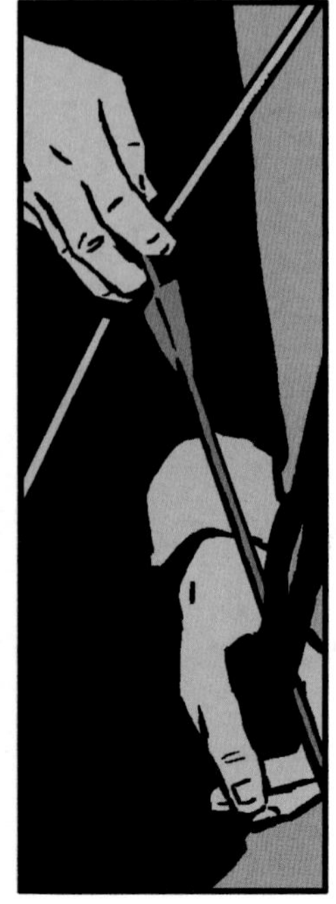

I NEED EVERYBODY'S HELP.

"...WE WENT OUT AND FOUND A LITTLE TROUBLE TONIGHT."
THE STUFF WHAT DON'T GET SPOKE
DAILY BUGLE
BY FRACTION AND AJA WITH HOLLINGSWORTH

20

AJA

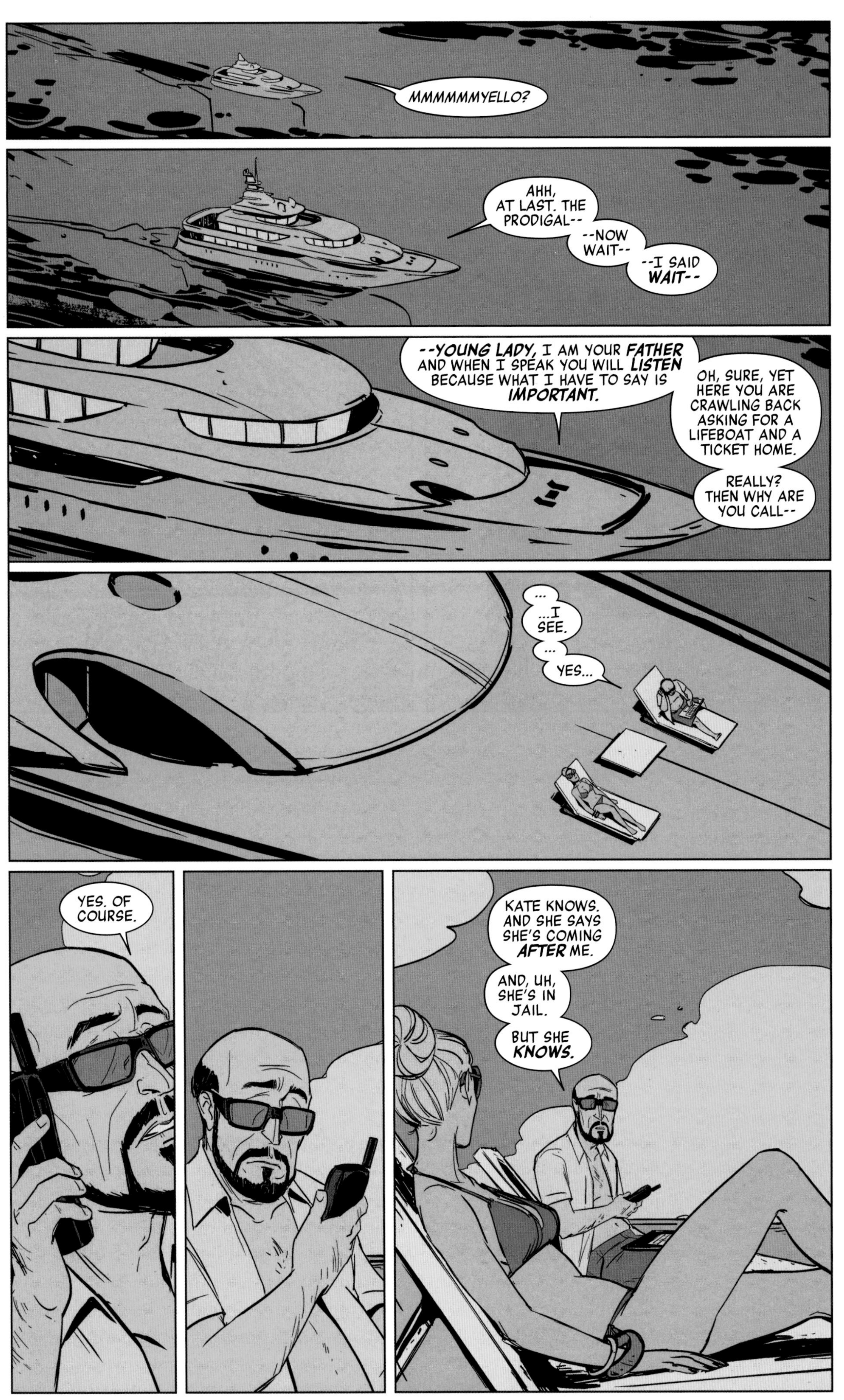
MMMMMMYELLO?
AHH, AT LAST. THE PRODIGAL--
--NOW WAIT--
--I SAID WAIT--
--YOUNG LADY, I AM YOUR FATHER AND WHEN I SPEAK YOU WILL LISTEN BECAUSE WHAT I HAVE TO SAY IS IMPORTANT.
OH, SURE, YET HERE YOU ARE CRAWLING BACK ASKING FOR A LIFEBOAT AND A TICKET HOME.
REALLY? THEN WHY ARE YOU CALL--
...
...I SEE.
...
YES...
YES. OF COURSE.
KATE KNOWS. AND SHE SAYS SHE'S COMING AFTER ME.
AND, UH, SHE'S IN JAIL.
BUT SHE KNOWS.

"WHEN DO I GET MY PHONE CALL?"

"PLEASE TURN BACK--"

WANTS TO DO GOO
heap rates - Great Results - Light Housekeeping
LIKE I SAID, THEY STOLE MY LIKENESS--
"THEY." THE CARD PEOPLE.
BIG GREETING.
HE'S CHEATING ON ME.
"HE"?! FOR REAL?
BECAUSE I WAS LIKE TOTALLY SWIPING RIGHT OVER HERE.
BAD ENOUGH SHE STOLE MY LOOKS AND MY LIFE--
--BUT THEN SHE STOLE MY STUFF AND I--
MM. PASS.
ESTEBAN IS TRYING TO KILL ME BECAUSE OF MY BLOG.
PRETTY BAD BLOG THEN, HUH.
YOU CALLED ME.
I FOUND A CAR.
I CAN DRIVE IT HOME AND SAVE MY FRIEND FROM THE BAD GUYS.
LOAN ME TWO GRAND?
WUHHZ-- WHAT. HELLO. HELLO. WHAT.
KATE BISHOP INVESTIGATIONS.
HI?

KATE BISHOP INVESTIGATIONS.
HI?

OH, IS THIS YOUR THING NOW? PRANK CALLS AND KEEPING ME--

SHINY-FACED SKANK HUNG UP ON ME.

SIGH

HEY, YOU.
NO, WHAT TIME IS IT THERE? WAIT, IT'S LIKE TWO HERE, SO--FIVE.
YEAH, OKAY, IT'S A LITTLE EARLY.
NO, WAIT, DON'T HANG UP IT'S BEEN LIKE FOREVER--

OKAY IT'S BEEN A COUPLE MONTHS. I JUST--
I MISS ALL YOU GUYS SINCE WE STOPPED HANGING OUT.
FINE, SINCE I LEFT.
I'M SO...LOST OUT HERE. AND I GOT BAD NEWS FROM HOME AND GOTTA SCRAMBLE BACK AND--

KNOCK KNOCK.
--NO I CAN'T JUST KICK ITS FACE OFF--
HANG ON.

KATE BISHOP?
YOU'RE UNDER ARREST.
"WAIT WAIT WAIT. BACK UP A SECOND..."

...WHAT MAKES YOU TWO THINK I'D JUST REVEAL CONFIDENTIAL CLIENT INFORMATION--
BECAUSE YOU REVEALED IT TO US, GARY.
AND NOW YOU SHOULD REVEAL IT TO HER.

=SIGH= FINE.
I HAVE A NEW CLIENT, IS ALL. VERY MONIED. VERY...PRIVATE.

"SHE BUYS ALL MY ORCHIDS EXCLUSIVELY NOW. AND OTHER EXOTICS.

"SHE RUNS SUSHI GIRL PARTIES. SOME KIND OF WEIRD BUSINESS THING. YOU KNOW WHAT I MEAN?
"PRETTY GIRLS LIE THERE WHILE GROSS OLD GUYS EAT SASHIMI OFF OF THEM?"

HER NAME'S WHITNEY FROST AND SHE--
WAIT.

SHE'S A STRAIGHT-UP SUPER VILLAIN, YO.

AND FLYNT-WARD-THE-WEED-LORD WHO SHOOK YOU DOWN AND BURNED YOUR SHOP--
--WAS ON HER PAYROLL. GET IT?

WARD. FROST. AND YOU, THE SUCKER IN THE MIDDLE.

SHE...
SHE'S THE ONE WHO TORCHED MY SHOP?

NEVER FEAR.
IF YOU'RE IN, BRINGING DOWN FROST IS PRACTICALLY A KATE ACCOMPLI.
SEE BECAUSE MY NAME IS KATE AND I--

--LOOKS GOOD ENOUGH TO EAT, DOESN'T SHE, GENTLEMEN?

BON APPÉTIT!
GARY, THAT'S YOUR CUE.
--YES, MA'AM, SORRY, MA'AM--
GENTLEMEN, THIS LAST QUARTER OUR PROFITS WERE UP BEYOND EXPECTATIONS FOR THE TWENTY-FIRST QUARTER IN A ROW.
YOU MANAGED TO MAKE THIS COMPANY A FORTUNE ON BOTH SIDES OF A GLOBAL RECESSION.
BUT THEY CALL ME THE SUPER VILLAIN.
AS A TOKEN OF MY GRATITUDE FOR YOUR HARD WORK AND DILIGENCE IN THE PAST QUARTER, THIS GIRL--
AH.
"HOLD ON."
I PUT MY LIFE ON THE LINE AND SMUGGLE YOU INTO THE OFFICES OF THE MOST DANGEROUS WOMAN IN LOS ANGELES. SURE OKAY.
BUT YOU--
HOW CAN YOU BE SURE YOU CAN GET HER PULLED OUT OF THE ROOM AT PRECISELY THE RIGHT TIME?
"HAROLD H. HAROLD WAS FOUND DEAD WITH YOUR ARROW IN HIS CHEST."

WHAT'S A NICE GIRL LIKE YOU--
YEAH, YEAH. DON'T I GET A PHONE CALL OR SOMETHING?

MEH.

CHARGE ME, GIVE ME A PHONE CALL, OR GET ME MY LAWYER. I KNOW MY RIGHTS.
ALSO MY DAD IS RICH AND HIS LAWYER HAS THE TMI GUYS ON SPEED-DIAL.
POLICE DEPT
A MONICA, C.A.
59640
BISHOP, K.

=SIGH=

CAUDLE.

COME ON, MAN.

YOU KNOW I DIDN'T DO IT. YOU HAVE ME ON TRAFFIC CAMS AT THE AIRPORT AND ON MY WAY TO THE PRECINCT.

THERE WAS LITERALLY NO TIME FOR ME TO COMMIT THE CRIME BEFORE SHOWING UP HERE THAT NIGHT.
AND WHY KILL MY FRIEND THEN COME HERE IMMEDIATELY?

WHAT YOU HAVE IS CIRCUMSTANTIAL AT BEST.
SO WHY ARE YOU GUYS HOLDING ME?

SIR, THIS JUST--
JONESY, COME ON, FACES AND SPACES, PAL, REMEMBER?
NOW WHAT'S SO--

=SIGH=
MS. BISHOP, SOMEONE JUST POSTED YOUR BAIL AND YOU'RE FREE TO GO.
DON'T LEAVE TOWN.

ACTUALLY I TAKE IT BACK PLEASE LEAVE TOWN.
FOREVER.

AWW, YOU GUYS--

--YOU'RE THE BEST. THANK YOU SO--
AH-AH, SWEETIE, NOT US.
HOP IN BACK.

WELL, THANK YOU, MYSTERIOUS BENEFACTOR--

HEY, KID.
HABEAS CORPUS, HUH?

AW, JEEZ--
"SEE, KID, IT WAS ALWAYS ABOUT BODIES...

"DEAD, ALIVE.
"YOUNG AND OLD.
"MOSTLY YOUNG. IT IS LOS ANGELES, RIGHT...?"

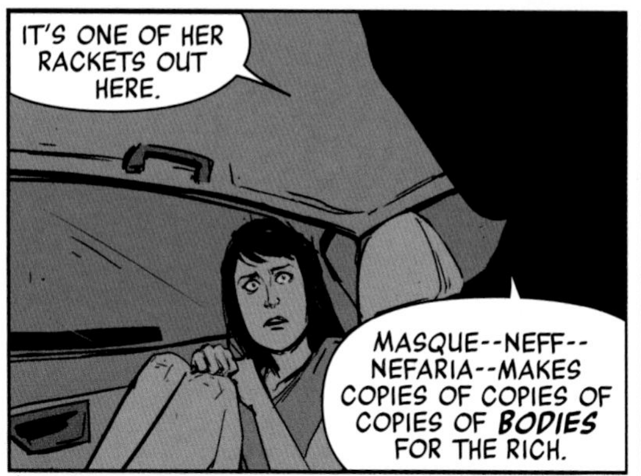
IT'S ONE OF HER RACKETS OUT HERE.
MASQUE--NEFF--NEFARIA--MAKES COPIES OF COPIES OF COPIES OF BODIES FOR THE RICH.

THIS IS SOME REAL S.H.I.E.L.D. STUFF. THEY USED TO CALL THEM LIFE MODEL DECOYS. OR--
--OR THE TECHNOLOGY ANYWAY. I THINK THE NEFFS STOLE IT. OR BOOTLEGGED IT.
IT'S SOME REAL VAMPIRE CRAP.

BUT YOU DIED.
CAN I TOUCH YOUR FACE? ARE YOU REALLY REAL?

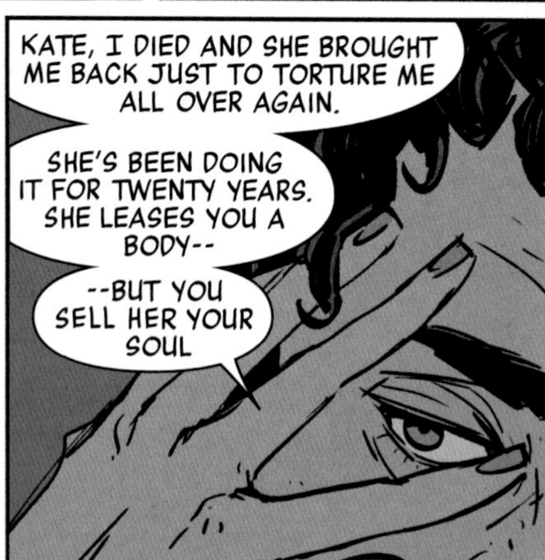
KATE, I DIED AND SHE BROUGHT ME BACK JUST TO TORTURE ME ALL OVER AGAIN.
SHE'S BEEN DOING IT FOR TWENTY YEARS. SHE LEASES YOU A BODY--
--BUT YOU SELL HER YOUR SOUL

HONEY, WE ACTUALLY HAVE SOME GOOD NEWS.
DO YOU REMEMBER OUR FLORIST FRIEND? YOU'LL NEVER GUESS WHO HE'S WORKING FOR THESE DAYS...

IT SEEMED PRETTY SIMPLE.

LIKE THE KIND OF THING I COULD HANDLE, RIGHT?
MY FLORIST FRIEND WOULD SNEAK ME INTO MASQUE'S HEADQUARTERS AS THE SUSHI GIRL.
AND I'D-- I'D--

I'M SORRY-- GIMME A SECOND--

TICK TOCK, HAROLD. WHAT'S BROUGHT YOU OUT OF THE GRAVE AND TO MY OFFICES THIS TIME?
"HE CHANGED HIS MIND, HE SAID.
"HE SAID SEEING SOMEONE LIKE ME CARE SO MUCH...HE WAS READY TO FIGHT BACK, FINALLY.
"SO I'D PLAY SUSHI GIRL AND HAROLD WOULD GET HER OUT OF THE ROOM. THEN I'D..."

...THEN I'D GO LOOKING FOR INCRIMINATING EVIDENCE.

EVERY LAST ONE OF YOU SIT THE FUTZ DOWN AND SHUT THE FUTZ UP RIGHT **NOW.**
AS SOON AS I WIPE THE SALMON ROE FROM MY NETHERS I'LL BE GETTING MY COSTUME ON AND TAKING MY LEAVE OF YOU CREEPS.
I CATCH ANY OF YOU **LOOKING** AND I'LL HAVE MYSELF THE VERY EYE WHAT SNUCK THE PEEK. ARE WE CLEAR?
YOU SHOULD BE ASHAMED...
...I'M OLD ENOUGH TO BE YOUR DAUGHTER'S...
...SUPER COOL AND JUST-A-LITTLE-BIT-WORLDLY...
zzZIP
...YOUNGER, **AWESOME,** FRIEND.
"GETTING IN AND GETTING ON WITH IT WASN'T HARD.
"I FIGURED WE HAD FIVE MINUTES MAX."
I JUST HAD TO FIND EVIDENCE HAROLD COULD PUT IN HIS STORY. BACKERS, CLIENTS, SUPPLIES, ANYTHING.
SOME KIND OF PAPER TRAIL THAT WAS MORE THAN JUST HIM, HE SAID.
"HAROLD WOULD KEEP HER BUSY SO I COULD GET TO SNEAKING.
"THEN I'D SLIP OUT AND HE'D GET TO REPORTING."

AND I FOUND IT. ALL RIGHT THERE, SECOND OR THIRD TERMINAL I TRIED.
IT WAS LIKE THEY WERE SO SURE NOBODY COULD STEP TO THEM THEY'D STOPPED PREPARING FOR IT.

BARTON, OH MY GOD THIS IS SO USELESS--

USB ARROW, KATE. 256 MEGS OF DATA ON THIS SWEET BABY. THAT'S LIKE FOUR AND A HALF WHOLE ALBUMS.
OR, LIKE, DOZENS OF PHOTOGRAPHS.
OR REALLY IMPORTANT TAX RECORDS AND--

--CLIENT DIRECTORIES WITH BANK CODES, ROUTING NUMBERS... A GOLD MINE.
BUT YOU ALREADY KNOW THAT, DON'T YOU.

YES, MS. BISHOP.
WE DO.

WELL, I DIDN'T.

CLIENT
BISHOP
DEREK
ADDRESS
"I DIDN'T KNOW ANYTHING AT ALL."

"SO THE JIG WAS UP. NO BIGS.

--AAAH, PHIL, SHE GOT ME SHE GOT ME--
"SO I MAYBE UNDERESTIMATED THE BASIC HERO-TO-GOON RATIO UP IN THAT PIECE.
"SINCE WHEN DOES AN AVENGER FLINCH FROM A SCRAP?"
"MS. BISHOP, YOU'RE NOT--"
"TECHNICALLY AN AVENGER, FINE. A YOUNG AVENGER, WHATEVER.
"I WON, DIDN'T I?
"I GOT OUT IN ONE PIECE.
"KINDA."

HER BUSINESS, IT'S ALL ABOUT BODIES. AND THIS THING OF OURS--
--SEE, WHITNEY FROST--MADAME MASQUE--HATES MY GUTS.

"I GOT THE JUMP ON HER ONCE UPON A TIME.
"SUPER HERO BUSINESS.

"I BEAT HER UP AND TIED HER UP AND PRETENDED TO BE HER BUT I NEVER LOOKED AT HER REAL FACE, RIGHT?
"I RESPECTED HER PRIVACY LIKE A DUMMY.

"AND SO ONE DAY SHE GOT THE DROP ON ME, RIGHT AFTER I MOVED OUT HERE.

"I GOT TO SEE WHERE SHE DID HER WORK...

"ONLY AT THE TIME I DIDN'T REALIZE WHAT I WAS SEEING.

"BODIES, RIGHT?
"HER OWN, HAROLD'S. THE BUILDING BLOCKS OF AN EMPIRE.
"A BUSINESS BUILT ON KEEPING THE VERY RICH YOUNG AND PRETTY.
"BETTER THAN BOTOX. MORE PERFECT THAN PLASTIC SURGERY."

"I MEAN, DO YOUR RESEARCH, RIGHT?
"MASQUE HERSELF GOT HER BRAINS BASHED OUT BY MOON KNIGHT ONE TIME BUT THEN GOT ALL BETTER.

"AND THAT'S HOW.
"ALSO THERE IS SOMEONE CALLED MOON KNIGHT OUT THERE IN THE WORLD. F.Y.I.

"ANYWAY I FIGURED WE HAD ALL THE DATA WE NEEDED, AND SHE BURNED MY PLACE DOWN, SO...

"...PAYBACK'S A BITCH."

OH, BROTHER.

"SO WHAT'S THE SCARIEST THING YOU'VE EVER SEEN IN YOUR WHOLE LIFE?
"BECAUSE A WALL OF WEIRD BURNING BELLBOY ZOMBIE FIGHT-AUTOMATONS IS NOW AT THE TOP OF MINE."

OH, SH--

--OT. HOT AND...AND STRONG.
ALL OF THEM. I WAS FROZEN AT FIRST. BUT THEN--

THEN THEY BEAT THE HELL OUT OF ME.
"MORE HUMAN THAN WHATEVER" OR WHATEVER. EXPLAINS A LOT.
HAROLD CALLED 'EM "LIFE MODEL DECOYS" WHICH DIDN'T MEAN ANYTHING TO ME--

--BUT IT MEANS A WHOLE HELL OF A LOT TO YOU, HUH.

WE CAN NEITHER CONFIRM NOR DENY THAT, MS. BISHOP.
WE'D RECEIVED A CREDIBLE TIP INFORMING US THAT MS. NEFF MERITED INVESTIGATION IS ALL.

YOU.
ME.

YOU--

"YOU GUYS SAVED MY LIFE."

SO THANKS FOR THAT, YEAH?
AND, UH. THAT'S PRETTY MUCH MY STORY.
DID YOU ARREST HER? DID YOU GET HER?

I THINK WE'RE DONE HERE.

NO, NO, NO--
--WAIT--
-- DON'T SAY THIS WAS ALL FOR NOTHING.

OF COURSE IT WAS FOR SOMETHING, MS. BISHOP.

JUST NOT YOUR THING.

I'D LIKE TO CALL MY FATHER, PLEASE.

PLES
OR $3
DAY ONLY!
OPEN
24
hours
TOAST
BUY 1, GET 1
YOU SET ME UP!
SALE
DELI
FRESH!

YEAH, PRETTY MUCH.
I KNEW YOU'D BRING DOWN ALL KINDS OF TROUBLE THOUGH AND THAT'S WHAT I NEEDED MOST.

BUT--
--BUT--
--BUT I--
YOU--

I NEEDED A SUPER HERO TO SAVE MY LIFE.
AND THEN I NEEDED THE WRATH OF GOD TO SHUT DOWN NEFF ONCE AND FOR ALL.
A PIECE IN THE PAPER WASN'T GONNA DO IT, KATE.

THAT SUCKS!

AND YOU SUCK!
I DIDN'T GET TO BUST HER AT ALL!

AND S.H.I.E.L.D. SWOOPED IN AND COVERED IT ALL UP AND--

WHAT'S THE POINT OF ALL THIS, THEN?!

I CAME OUT HERE TO STAND ON MY OWN, TO BE A HERO, AND-- AND--
--AND THEY'RE GONNA LET HER OUT. AND THE BAD GUYS WIN OR AT LEAST DON'T GET PUNISHED AND--
--AND WHAT'S THE POINT? LOS ANGELES, THE BODIES, THE STUPID CAT FOOD--
FORGET IT, KATE.
IT'S A METAPHOR.

I HAD ONE JOB AND I DIDN'T DO IT.
ONE JOB.
SWEETIE...
HONEY...

SERIOUSLY, GUYS. IF I SUCKED, WOULD YOU TELL ME?

I GOT THOSE NICE LESBIANS' TRAILER BURNED DOWN, YOU GUYS HAVE TO TAKE HER AWFUL CAT--

AND I OWE YOU SO MUCH MONEY FOR THE CAR AND BAIL AND--

KATE BISHOP. STOP IT RIGHT NOW.

YOU SAVED OUR WEDDING. NOW GO SAVE YOUR FRIEND.
GO BE A SUPER HERO. YOU'RE A SUPER HERO TO US.

YOU GUYS ARE THE BEST.
I LOVE YOU SO MUCH. THANK YOU FOR EVERYTHING.
YOU'RE THE BEST FAMILY A GIRL COULD ASK FOR.
DAD. IT'S ME.

"OH SHUT IT. WE NEED TO--
"--NO--DAD, WE NEED TO TALK--
"WHY? YOU HAVE NOTHING TO SAY TO ME WORTH LISTENING TO.
"FATHER OF MINE, I AM BROKE AS A JOKE AND ACTUALLY IN JAIL SO I THINK I GOT YOU BEAT.
"YEAH, DON'T WORRY. THE LAST THING I'LL BE DOING IN THIS LIFE IS TO TAKE MONEY OR HELP FROM YOU EVER AGAIN. AND JAIL IS THE ONLY THING KEEPING ME FROM YOU RIGHT NOW.
You Are Now Leaving
Los Angeles
"DAD, I RAN INTO GIULINA NEFF OUT HERE.
"I'M SAYING I KNOW, DAD. I KNOW ABOUT YOU. AND I AM GOING TO MAKE YOU PAY. AND PAY AND PAY AND PAY.
"NOT IF I SEE YOU FIRST. I'M COMING HOME. AND I'M GONNA SAVE MY FRIEND'S LIFE. AND THEN?"
THEN YOU AND ME ARE GOING TO HAVE WORDS.
HAWKEYE OUT.

21
AJA

"(IS THAT MINE?)"
"YEAH.
"...SOME OF IT ANYWAY."
THE REST...
"...OTHER BAD GUYS."
NOT THE TRACKSUIT DRACULAS. MY BAD GUYS, I MEAN. FROM THE DAY JOB.
THE TRACKSUITS DON'T KNOW OR DON'T CARE ABOUT IT ANYWAY.
"THEY JUST WANT THE BUILDING.
"...AND ALL OF US OUT OF IT."
YOU CAN WALK AWAY.
ER--I MEAN--
"--I'M SAYING, IF YOU'RE IN, OKAY--
"BUT IF THINGS GO SIDEWAYS..."
...YOU CAN TRY BUYING YOUR WAY OUT.
AND IF YOU'RE THINKING YOU'LL JUST TAKE IT WHEN MY BACK IS TURNED AND THAT SQUARES US?
I'LL HUNT YOU DOWN AND KILL YOU WITH MY BARE HANDS.
YOU'RE MY BROTHER AND I LOVE YOU AND I KNOW IF I'M IN IT, YOU'RE GONNA BE IN IT WITH ME ALL THE WAY.
YOU WERE THE GUY THAT TAUGHT ME THAT, BARN.
SO SCREW ME ON THIS ONE AND I'LL FUTZING END YOU, MAN.
LET'S GET TO WORK.

"RIO BRAVO"

BY MATT FRACTION AND DAVID AJA WITH RAUL ALLEN · MATT HOLLINGSWORTH · CHRIS ELIOPOULOS

DID. IT'S WHAT I DID.
Y'KNOW. BEFORE.

ANYTHING TO MAKE PEOPLE STOP CARING. ASK BOBBI. ASK--
NOTHING'S GONNA EXCUSE IT BUT I WANT YOU TO UNDERSTAND IT. AND--
--AND I WANT YOU TO UNDERSTAND THAT...I UNDERSTAND IT?

(WHAT'S SO DIFFERENT BETWEE(T?)[N] THEN AND (NEW?) [NOW?])
(YOU GET YOUR HEAD STABBED IN AND A (SWATS FLIES?) (?/?) SOMEWHERE?)

I...
I SAW BARNEY AND THOSE KIDS NEXT DOOR.

I--IF HE-- JESS, MY OLD MAN, HE--
I THINK I WANT TO BE THE PERSON ALL OF YOU PEOPLE SEEM TO THINK I AM.

I DIDN'T BEFORE BUT I DO NOW.

(ARE YOU STARING AT ME LIKE THAT BECAUSE YOU'RE READING MY LIPS OR BECAUSE YOU WANT TO KISS ME?)

I'M SORRY I HURT YOU.
I'M SORRY I HIT YOU.

Incoming call

(WORK.)

"YOU GO.
"THEY DON'T NEED ME."

(CLINT...)

(YOU ARE SO WRONG ABOUT THAT.)

JUST GOTTA WRAP STUFF UP HERE, S'ALL.
WE'LL BE FINE.

Besides...

How much worse can it get?

"THIS IS GONNA GET REAL FUTZIN' BAD, BABY.
"I KNOW ALL ABOUT THE KIND OF MEN COMING FOR US...

"BECAUSE I USED TO BE JUST LIKE THEM.

"AND A BUNCH OF PRANKS WARMED OVER FROM *'HOME ALONE'* AIN'T GONNA GET IT DONE, SIMONE."

TWENTY-FOUR HOURS, GIVE OR TAKE. IF I'M NOT AT THE HARBOR IN--
YOU ***WILL BE.*** DON'T WORRY ABOUT IT.

YOU'LL BE FINE.
DON'T BE DUMB.
OKAY.

JUSSSSST...
...GONNA TAKE OUT A WHOLE BUNCHA BAD GUYS FIRST.

LIKE HELL YOU ARE.

UMPF
BECAUSE YOU'RE GONNA BE
UMPF
UP ON THE ROOF WHERE IT'S
UMPF
SAFE.

(WHAT ABOUT "IF I'M IN IT YOU'RE--")
YOU CAN'T MOVE, DUMMY.

YEAH, WELL, YOU'RE DEAF.

HOW'S IT LOOKIN' DOWN THERE, GIL'S DAD?

DEKE!
AIMEE!
GO!

Please PLEASE don't get yourselves killed.
KING

BE SAFE, YEAH? BUCKLE UP.
YEAH, MAN. YOU TOO.
KING

I GOTTA GET OUT OF THIS FUTZIN' CITY...

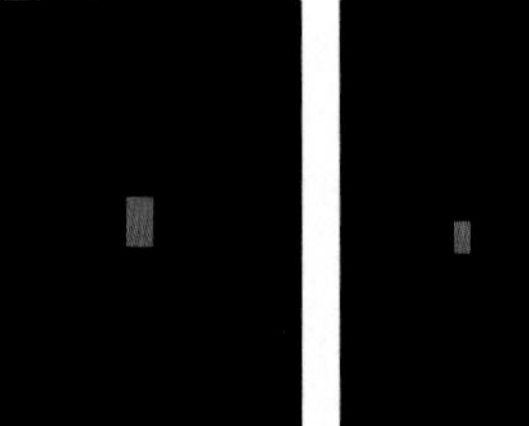

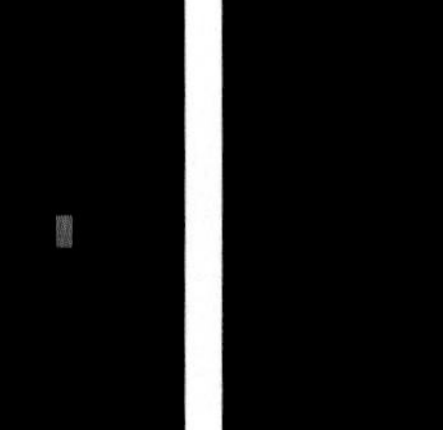

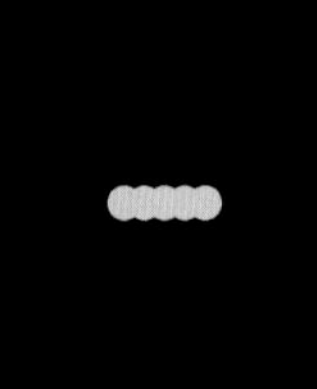

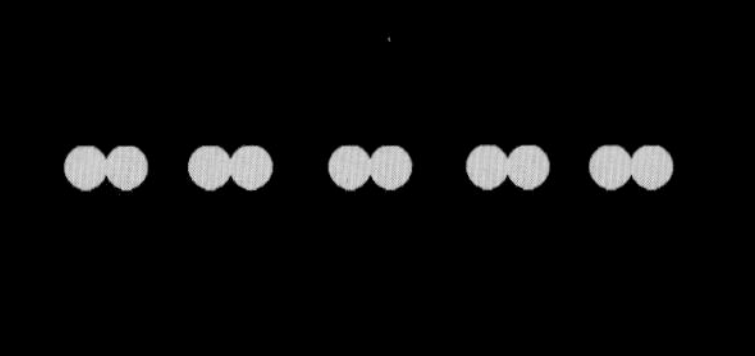

"OKAY BROS..."

BARTON IS ON TOP FLOOR.

SAFE IS ON TOP FLOOR TOO, BROS.

GO.

OHHHHH GOD.
I'M AN ARCHITECT WHAT AM I

SORRY CLINT

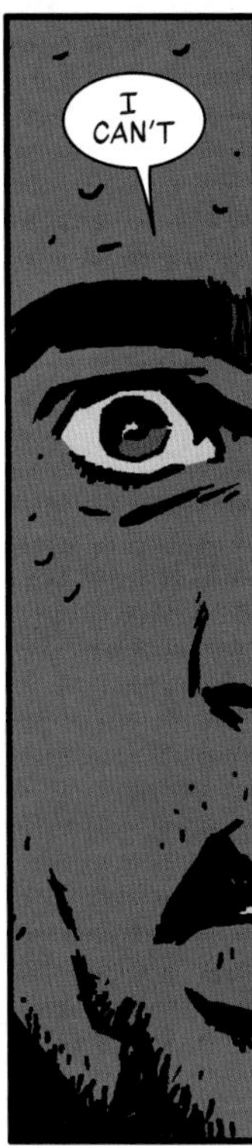
I CAN'T

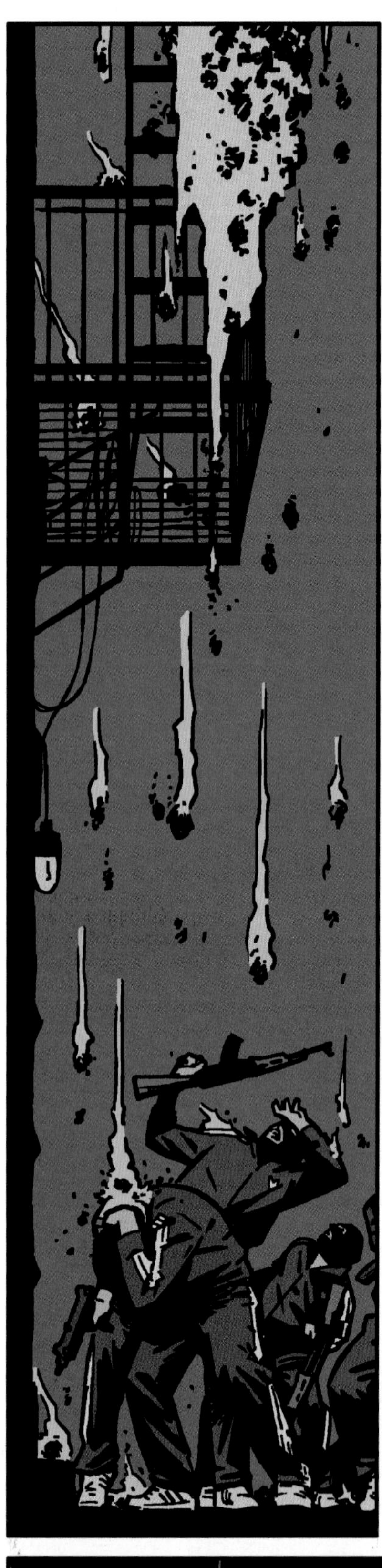

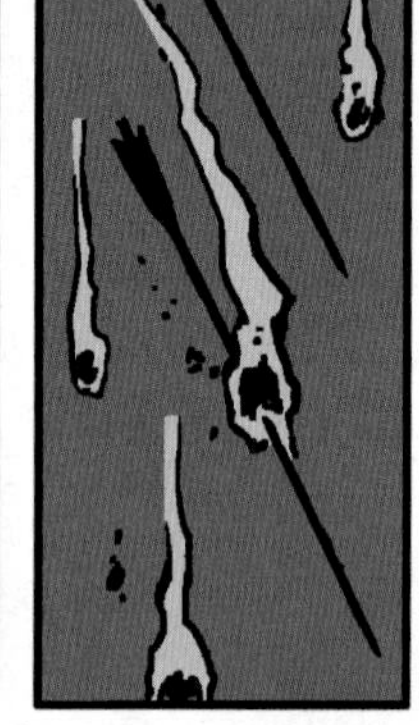

KILL THEM BROS NOW!!!

And that's how the battle of Bed-Stuy began.

THEY'RE HERE.

I PANICKED. I JUST LOCKED THE DOOR AND--
BE COOL, MAN.
JUST STICK TO THE PLAN.

"JUST STICK TO THE PLAN...

"AND IT'LL ALL BE COOL.

CLACK

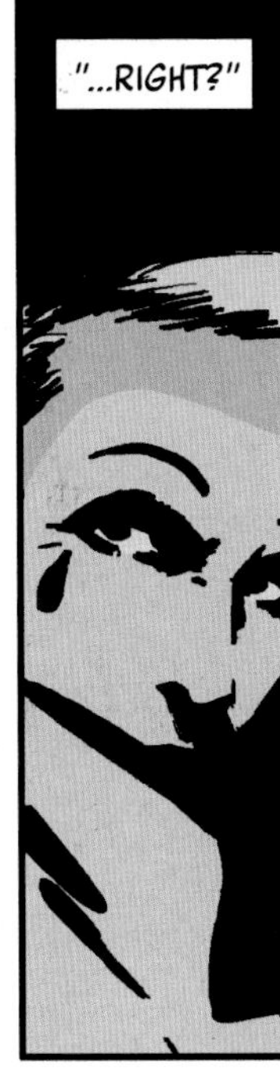
"...RIGHT?"

EASY MAN--
--I GOT THAT--

--MENDEL'S, MAN--

WHAT?

IS BARRICADE, BROS!

FUTZING BARTON.

HEFF.
HEFF.
HEFF.

KING

OHHHH MOMMA.

GO, BRO, GO!
GOING, BRO, GOING!

...BRO?

Okay, this...
...this looks like it's actually working.
Aimee's bottled 'em up at the front.

And everybody's old junk has 'em trapped in the stairwell.
BRO BRO BRO BARRICADE BRO
BRO

Not junk. Stuff.
And you gotta make your own stuff wor--

BLAMM BLAMM

HOW does he keep GETTING IN--

BRO--

CLACK

BLAMM
BRAKABRAKABRAKABRAKAB
BLAMM

CLACK
BLAMM

BLAMM

Get to the roof--
--get him away from--

--gotta lead him away from my nei--

YOU--
YOU--

--СВОЛОЧЬ--

YOU

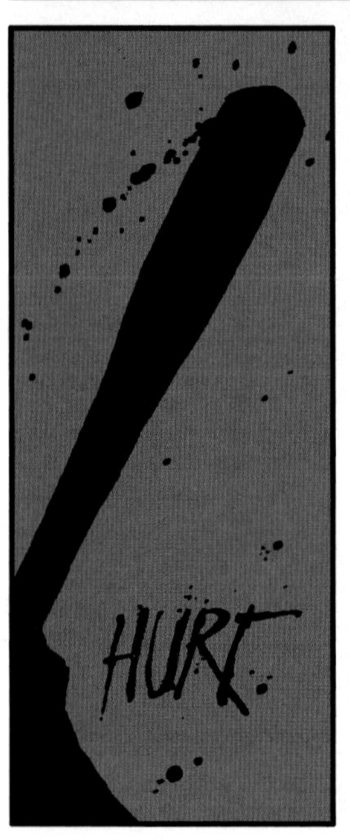
HURT

MY

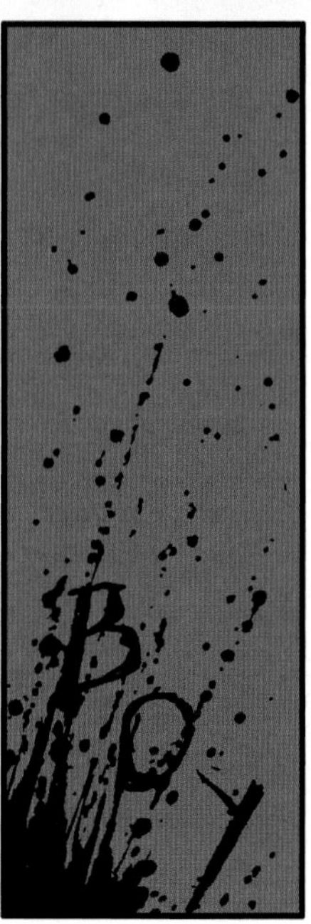
BOY

everything hurts

--EVERYTHING--

Barn
The MONEY, Bar--

Bar...uh...
Bar bar... bar...
CRAP can't tell what they're

Barney
Be safe

Safe?
What is Barney--
--YELLING--
SO MUCH YELLING about--

Why does HE want Barney
SAFE?
Oh WAIT--

GET OUT
Barney get

Did he
Are they
Barney
did you

SO TIRED
Jus' wanna
NAP an'

taught me
Barney
taught me

hit them until
they stop

Cap taught
me
Fighting
Barney
taught me
HURTING

Uh-oh
Barney's
gonna
know that look
Barney's gonna--

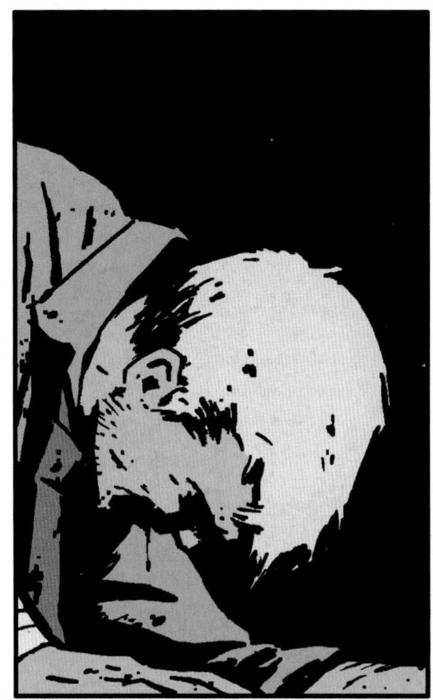

Barney's
gonna HURT

good

ol'
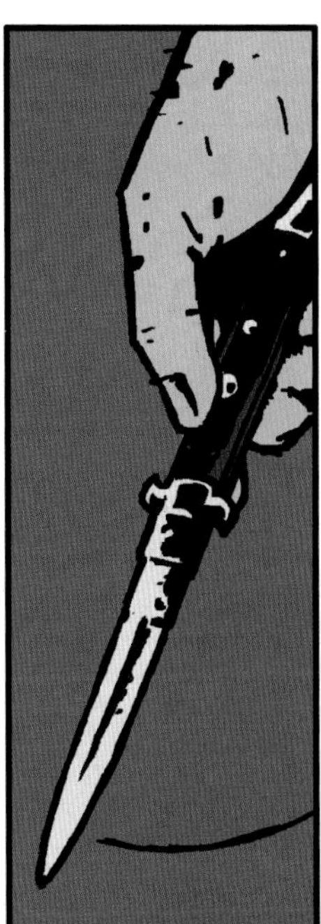

BARNEY

--UH-OH--

NOOOOOOOOOO

HEY
HEY
IT'S OKAY
IT'S
GUESS
GUESS WHAT

EXIT

22

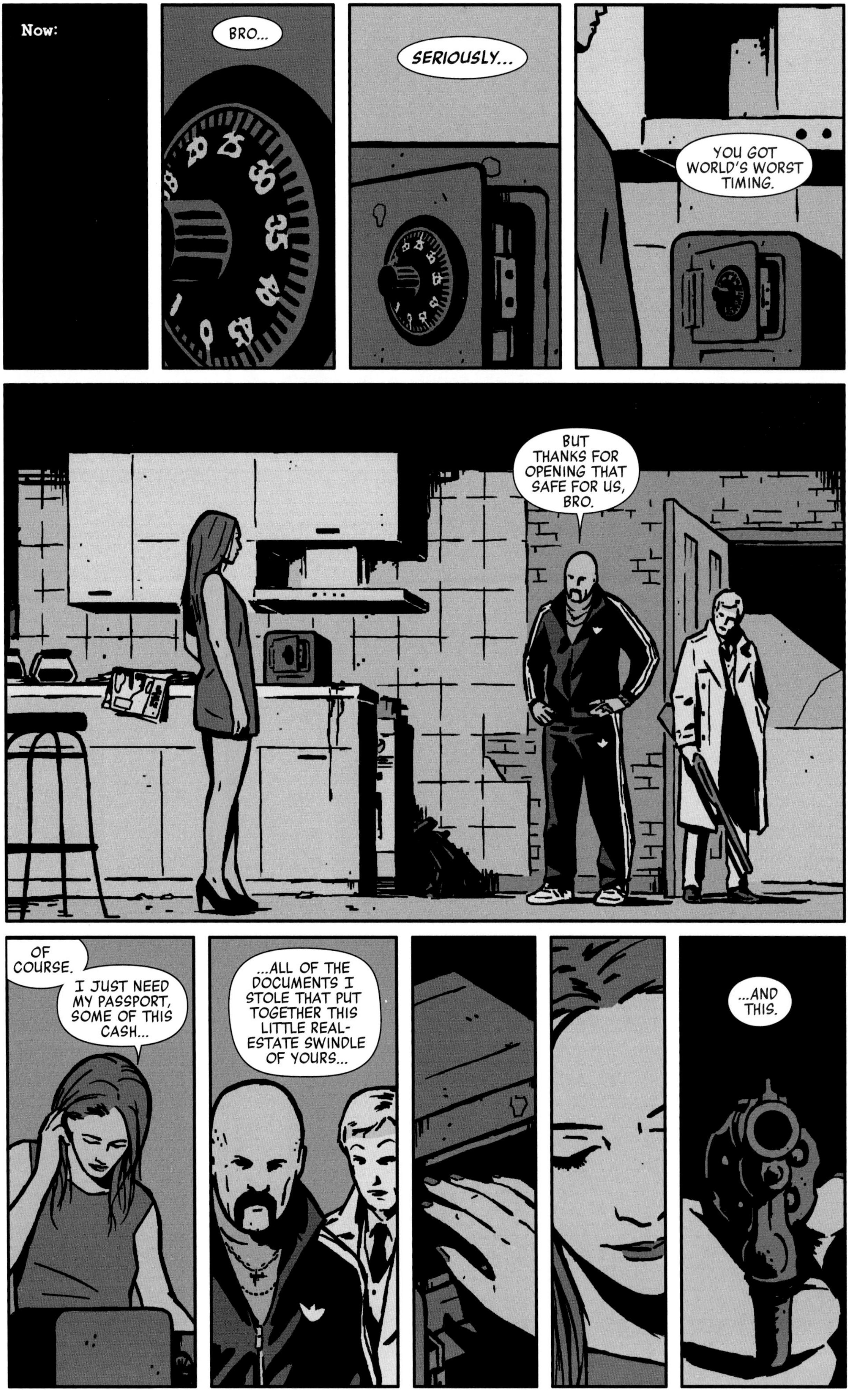

BUT THANKS FOR OPENING THAT SAFE FOR US, BRO.

I SHOT MY OWN HUSBAND WITH THIS, IVAN.
YOU THINK I WON'T SHOOT HIS BOSS?

TCCH.
BRO.

CLICK
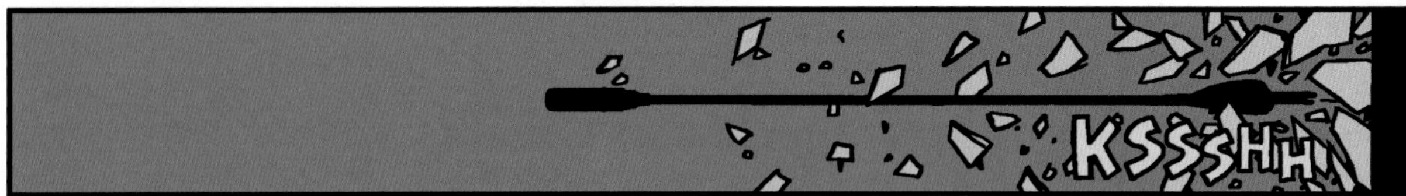
KSSSHH

TAP
...?

KASSHH

GET OUT OF MY APARTMENT.

CLACK

ROWF

AAAAAAAAA

BLAMM

WHERE THE FUTZ THIS FUTZING DOG FROM, BRO, WHERE--

CLINT...

(CURSE IN POLISH)

DON'T.
MOVE.

Just like ten minutes ago:

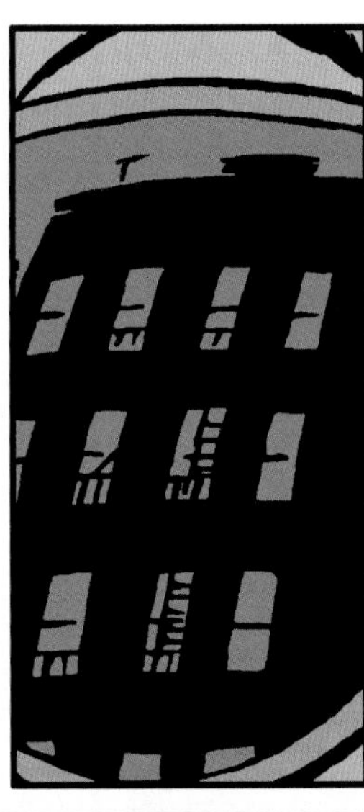

AIMEE?

STILL WITH US, KID?

UHN.
HEYYYY, HAWKEYE. WELCOME HOME.
WE BEAT THE BAD GUYS YET?

FIXIN' TO.
ЛАЙКА

OOF.
LIFT WITH *BACK,* BRO.

BRO, LOOK AT ALL THIS CRAP, BRO.
NEED DANG *DYNAMITE--*

TAP

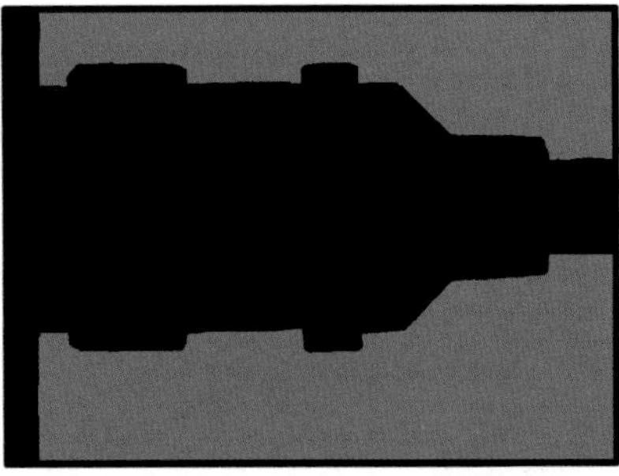

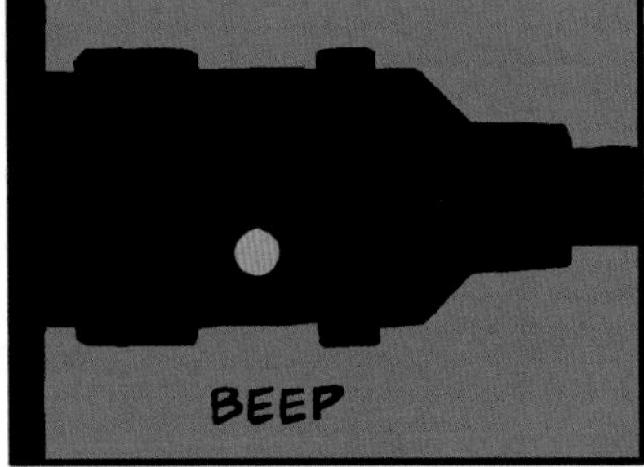
BEEP

KBOOM

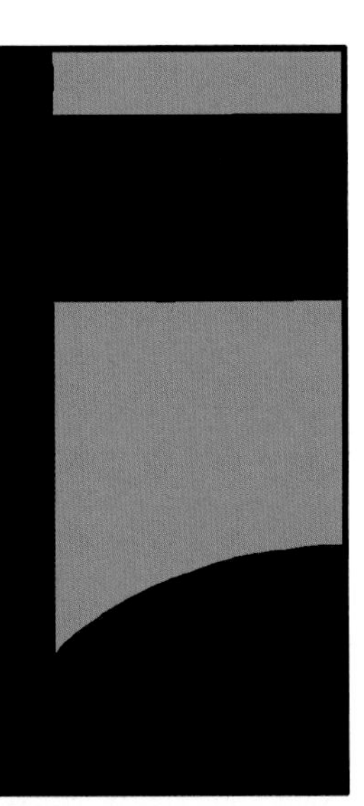

IT COMES BACK TO YOU IN THE END.

I AM RIGHT WAY MORE THAN YOU PEOPLE GIVE ME CREDIT FOR.

HOW YA DOIN' OVER THERE, HAWKEYE?

BREATHE OUT. BE COO--

WHMPP

KRAKK

GOOD DOG.
YOU'RE A *GOOD DOG.*
DON'T STOP FIGHTING, BOY.

WHOMPP

WHAKK

KRAKK

WHUKK

THWAKK

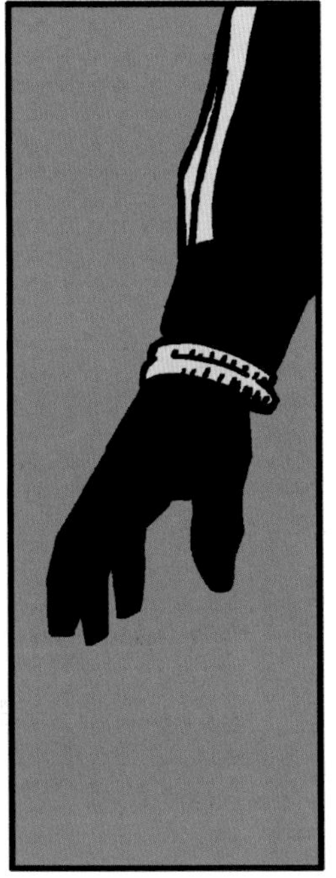

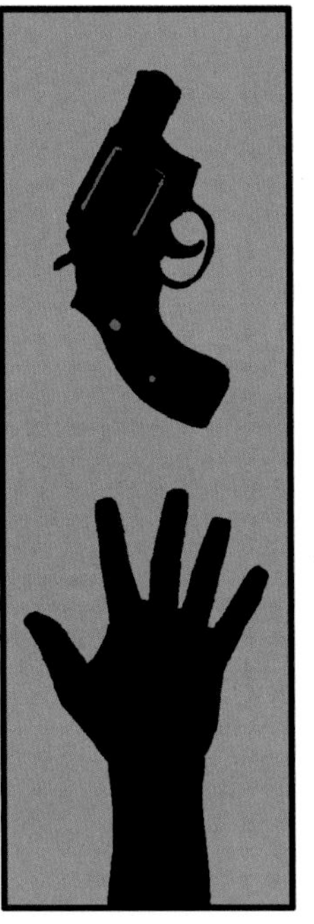

BLINK.
AND I SHOOT.

NOT AN EXIT

KEEP TRYING TO THINK WHY I SHOULDN'T DO IT.

AND?

AND I'M NOT LIKE YOU.
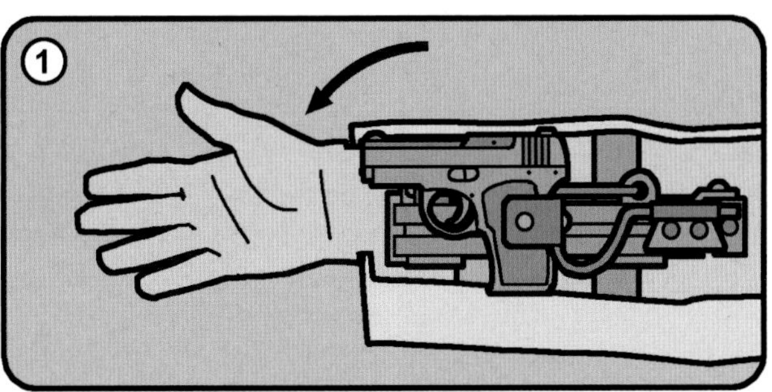
1
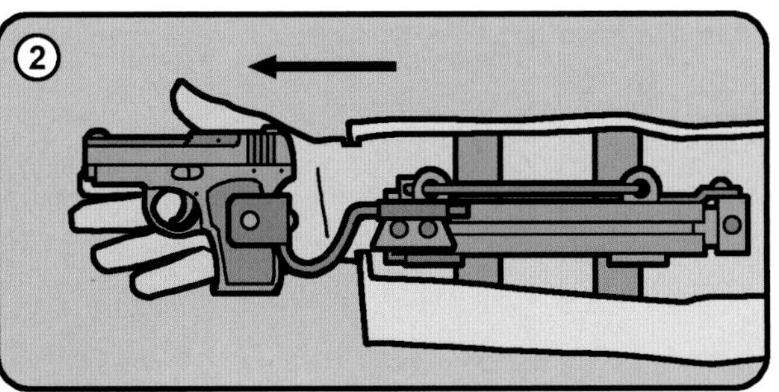
2

TOO BAD.

BLAM

ЛАЙКА

ALL I NEED IS MY CASH AND MY PASSPORT.
EVERYTHING CLINT NEEDS IS IN THAT SAFE, KATE.
I JUST WANT TO GET MY STUFF AND *GO.*

WHAT *"GO"*?
WHERE YOU THINK YOU GO, BRO, WE DON'T FIND YOU?

AND *YOU.*
GO AHEAD AND SHOOT ME, LADYBRO.

TOTALLY NOT THE NEGOTIATION TACTIC I EXPECTED HERE, TRACKSUIT DRACULA.

YOU TAKE *ME* OUT? NO.
GOTS LIKE ***SIXTEEN BROS*** DOWNSTAIRS.
MORE ACROSS CITY AND ***MORE*** MORE BACK HOME.

SHOOT HIM.
DON'T LISTEN TO HIM.
SHOOT HIM.

BE SUPER-SCARED RIGHT NOW IF IVAN WAS LADYBRO.

BECAUSE NONE MY BROS GOTS PROBLEMS SHOOTING LITTLE GIRLS.

NEIGHBORHOOD WATCH.
STAY DOWN.

MAN I FEEL SUUUUUUUPER-SKETCHY ABOUT SHOOTING SOMEBODY.
LET ALONE AN UNARMED D-BAG.
IT'S "STAND YOUR GROUND"!
A HOME INVASION! JUSTIFIABLE--

HERE.

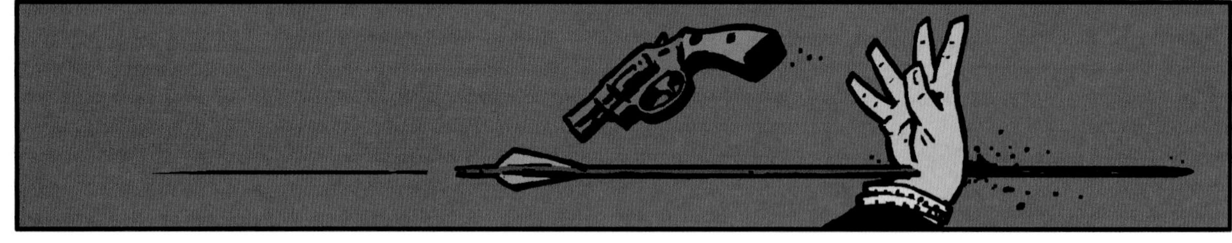

THAT WAS FOR THE DOG, YOU AWFUL SON OF A BITCH.

--=CLINT(?)=--
BLAMM

SNAP!

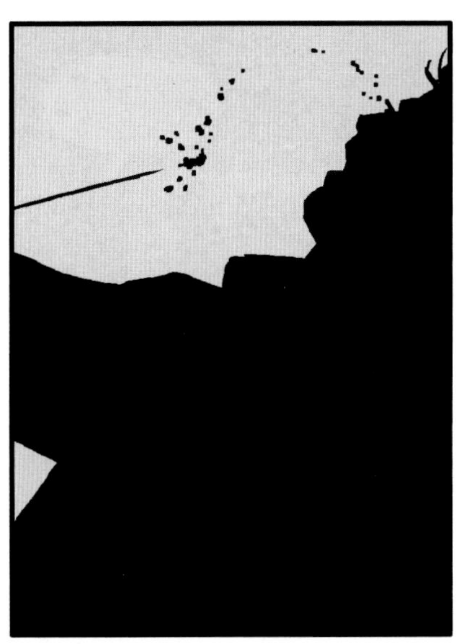

BUILDING'S NOT FOR SALE.

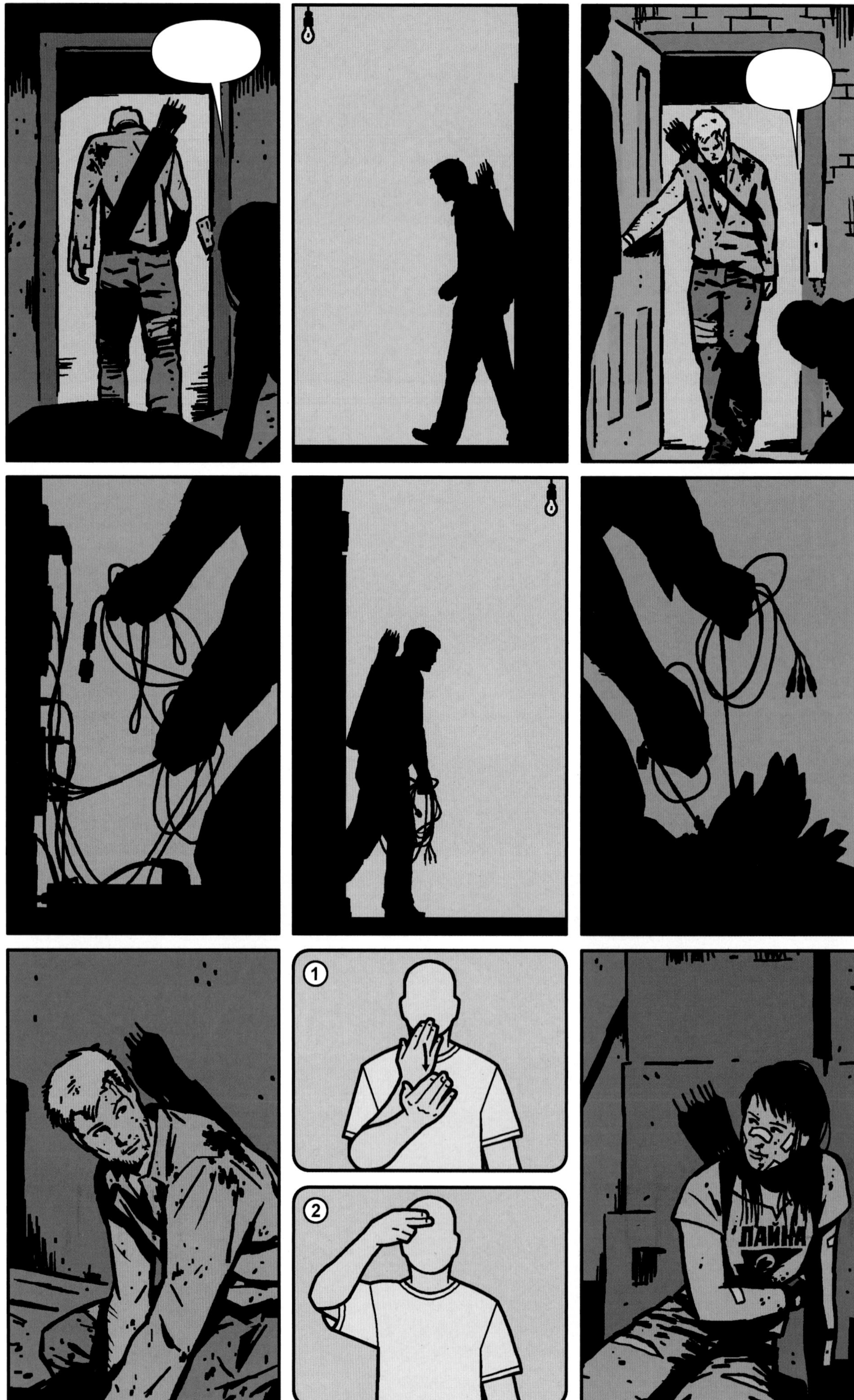
1
2
ЛАЙКА

WE GOT IT FROM HERE, HAWKEYE.
AN' THANKS.

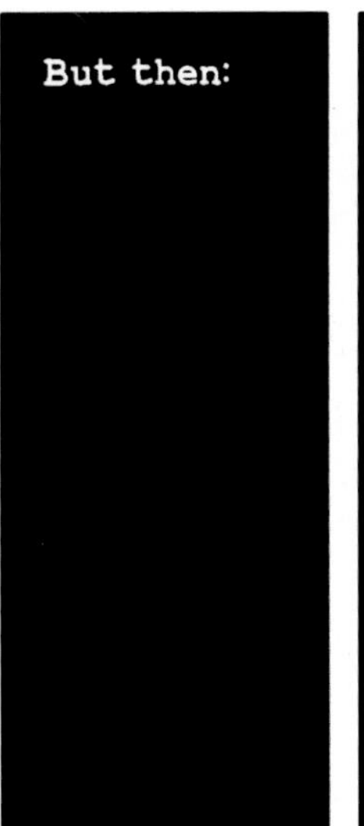
But then:

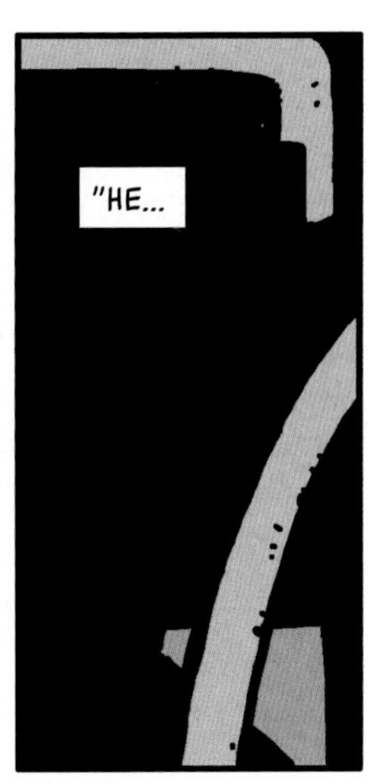
"HE...

"...HE WAS--

"--I *SWEAR* HE WAS RIGHT HERE."

AFTER YOU WENT BACK DOWN, HE STARTED MOVIN' AGAIN.
HE UNTIED ME.

SO THEN WHAT HAPPENED?
ЛАЙКА

WELL I *FIGURED* HE WAS OFF TO HELP YOU.

I'DA BET ALL MY MONEY HE--

--*MONEY.*

BARNEY *FUTZING* BARTON.

AND THE AVENGERS ARE COOL WITH THAT.

AND *HE'S* COOL WITH THAT. LIKE, FRAUD AND STUFF.

TCH.

OUR MARRIAGE WAS COMPLICATED.

TIME FOR THIS ONE TO GO.
SAY YOUR GOODBYES.

WELL...
WHOA.

BEST'A LUCK...UH.

YOU.

PENNY.

TIME TO GO BE SOMEBODY ELSE'S BAD LUCK, I GUESS.

"KILL THEM.
SUBJECT: Clint Barton
LAST NAME Barton
WEIGHT
York City Police
"BOTH OF THEM."

AGREED.

AGREED.

AGREED.

AGREED.

AGREED.

OUI.

AGREED.

WEIGHT

AGREED.

MR. BISHOP...?

WHAT SAY YOU?

AGREED.

WELL THEN, LADIES AND GENTLEMEN.

IT WOULD APPEAR WE ARE IN THE AVENGER-KILLING BUSINESS.

And THEN:

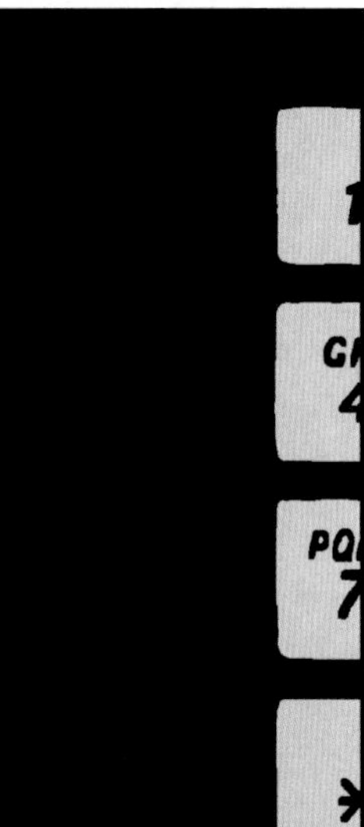

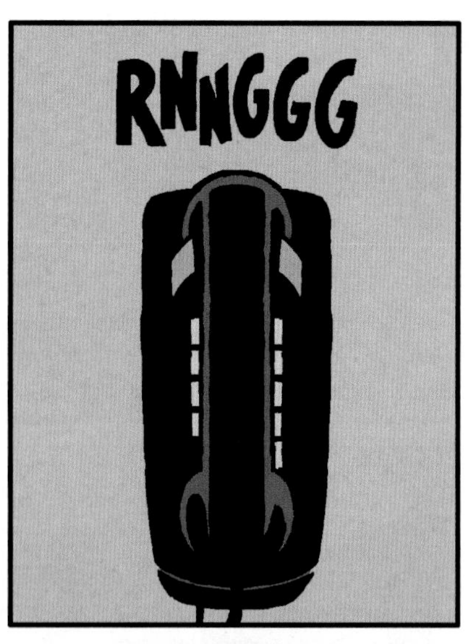

RNNGGG

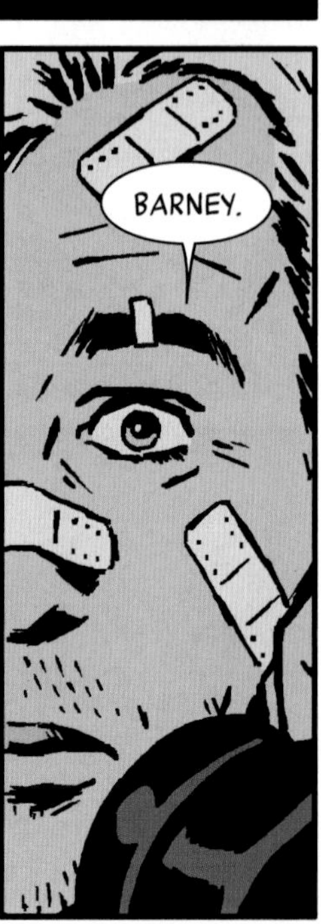

NO, DUMBASS, YOU SAY "CHICKEN-BUTT."
ONLY BEEN DOIN' THIS SINCE YOU WAS SIX...

SO, HEY, LISTEN--
I GOT MY MONEY BACK.

TOLD YOU A *LONNNNG* TIME AGO IT WAS GONNA HAPPEN AND NOW LOOK.
IT HAPPENED.
DIDN'T EVEN HAVE TO KILL YOU.

CLINT--CLINT CLINT CLINT *CLINT*--
--I DON'T CARE. I GOT SOME WOUNDS THAT GOTTA HEAL, SOME FANCY *MEALS* I WANNA EAT, I GOT A SPECIAL LADY TO TAKE NICE CARE OF--
--SSUURPP.

ALONG WITH THESE TWO LITTLE GOOFBALL BABIES OF HERS.
CHARLIE, OFF THE RAILING.
SORRY, UNCLE BARNEY.

THIS CASH WILL MORE THAN TAKE CARE OF US ALL FOR A NICE LONG TIME.
SO YOU TAKE IT EASY THERE, CLINT.

"I SWEAR TO GOD, BARNEY, I'M GONNA FIND YOU--"
"NO.
"YOU WON'T."

CLICK

...
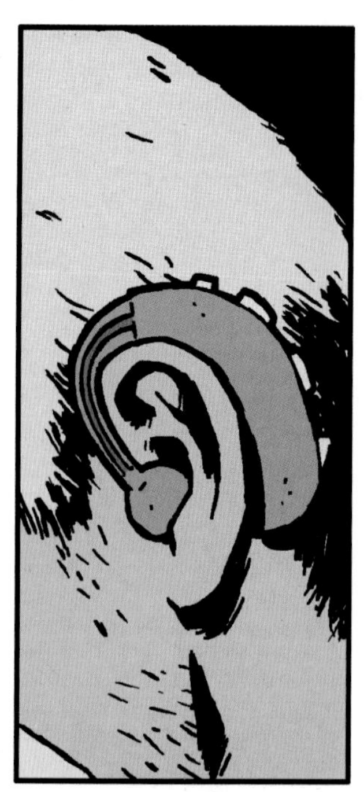

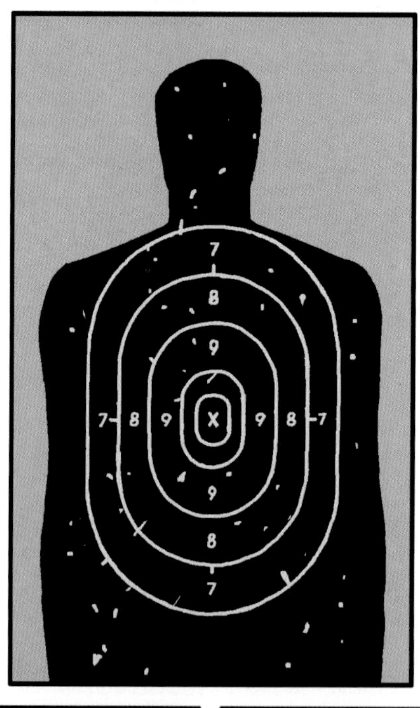
7
8
9
7 8 9 X 9 8 7
9
8
7

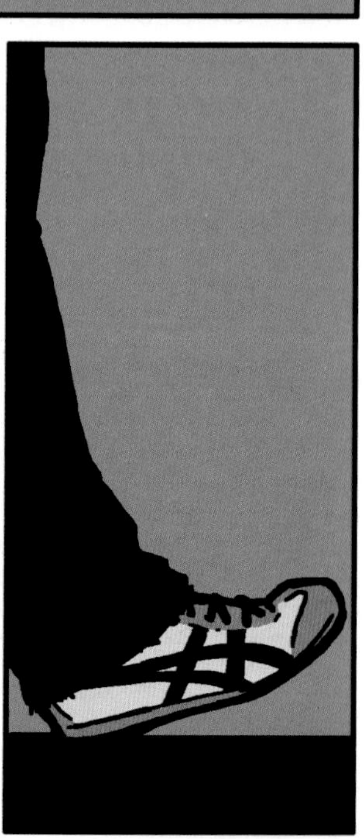

a
Clint Barton / Kate Bishop
Comic Book

by
Matt Fraction & David Aja

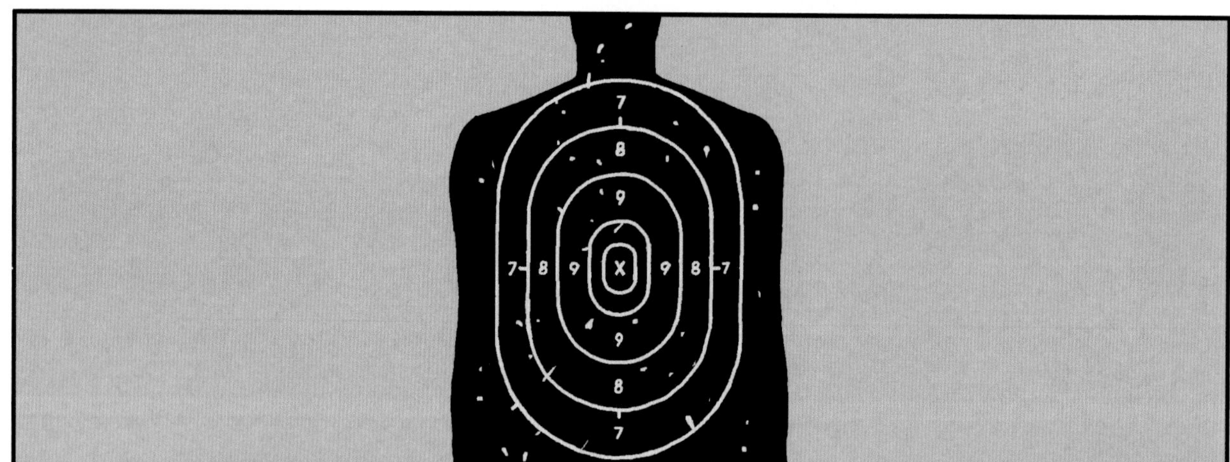

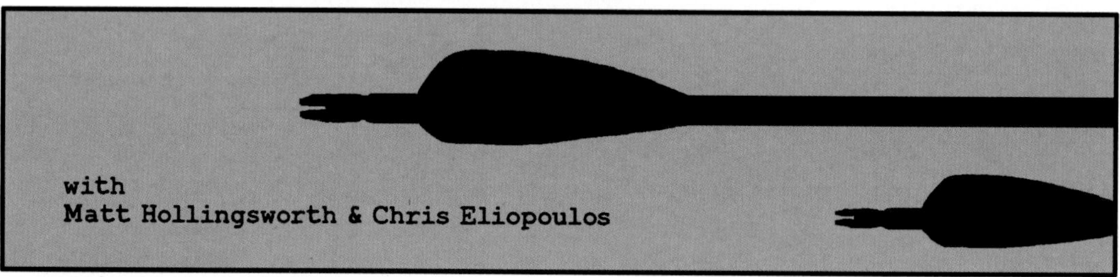
with
Matt Hollingsworth & Chris Eliopoulos

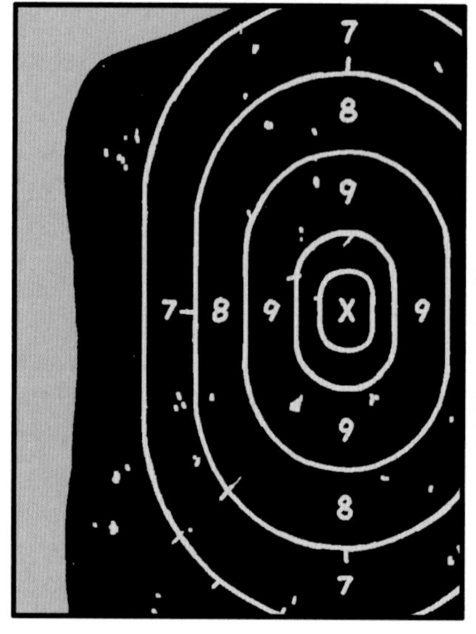

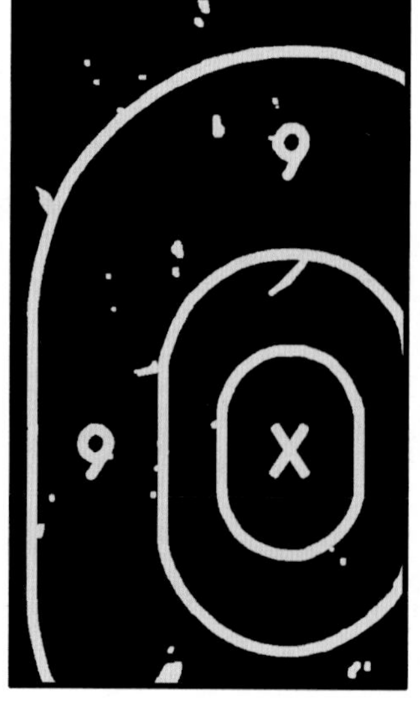

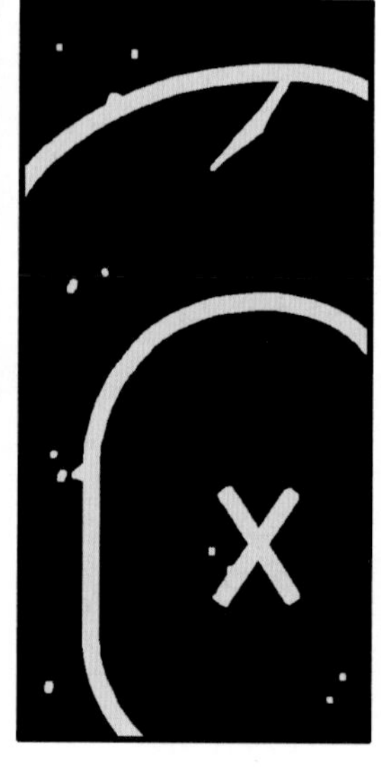

End.

ISSUE #13 COVER PROCESS
BY DAVID AJA

ISSUE 15, PAGE 20 LAYOUTS

ISSUE 15, PAGE 20 PENCILS

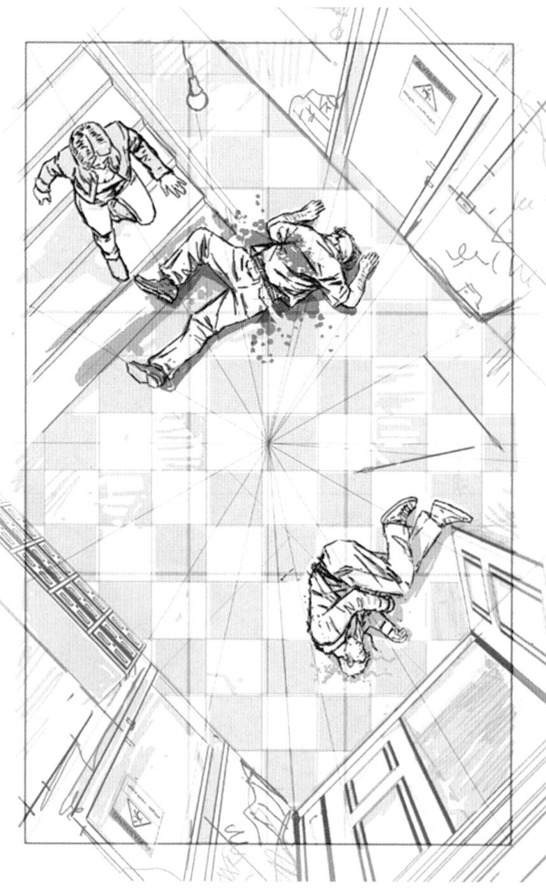

ISSUE 15, PAGE 20 FINAL

ISSUE 15, PAGE 20 PARTIAL INKS

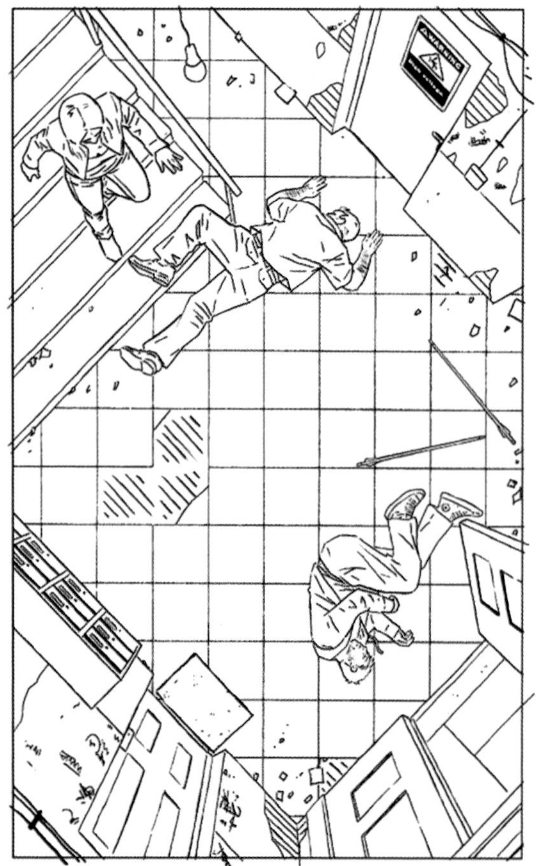

ISSUE 15, PAGE 20 INKS